LET THE
POET CHOOSE

D1327775

Let the Poet Choose

edited by

JAMES GIBSON

HARRAP LONDON

First published in Great Britain 1973
by GEORGE G. HARRAP & Co. LTD
182–184 High Holborn, London, W.C.1V 7AX

© James Gibson 1973

ISBN 0 245 51932 7 (boards)
      0 245 51934 3 (limp)

821.08
GIB

Printed in Great Britain by
WESTERN PRINTING SERVICES LTD, BRISTOL

THE POETS

Dannie Abse

Kingsley Amis

W. H. Auden

John Betjeman

Thomas Blackburn

Edmund Blunden

Alan Brownjohn

Charles Causley

Richard Church

Patric Dickinson

Lawrence Durrell

Clifford Dyment

Roy Fuller

Robert Gittings

Robert Graves

Thom Gunn

Seamus Heaney

John Heath-Stubbs

Philip Hobsbaum

David Holbrook

Ted Hughes

Elizabeth Jennings

James Kirkup

Philip Larkin

Laurie Lee

C. Day Lewis

Edward Lucie-Smith

George Macbeth

Roger McGough

Norman Nicholson

Brian Patten

Ruth Pitter

William Plomer

Peter Porter

Kathleen Raine

Anne Ridler

Vernon Scannell

Stevie Smith

Stephen Spender

Jon Stallworthy

R. S. Thomas

Anthony Thwaite

Charles Tomlinson

Ted Walker

PREFACE

'I feel, perhaps over-sensitively, that I am often mis-represented in anthologies.' Peter Porter's cry from the heart (page 132) illustrates very well one of the main reasons for *Let the Poet Choose*. Why should it always be the anthologist's choice of poems and never the poets'? Anthologies tend to beget anthologies, and the reader of anthologies might be excused for believing that Peter Porter had written only one poem—'Your Attention Please'.

The poems in this book have been chosen, therefore, not by me but by the poets themselves. This, for better or worse, is *their* anthology, begotten of them and not of other anthologies. The choice of poets was mine; the choice of poems is theirs. Each of the poets was asked to select two of his own poems which he would like to see included and to write a few lines about the reasons for the choice.

The result has been far more interesting and valuable than I could have hoped. Almost all the poets were keen and willing to contribute. Their notes, which have been published exactly as they wrote them, frequently reveal a fascinating insight into the nature of the creative process at work, and they tell us something about the poets themselves. The choice of poems is often as significant and self-revelatory.

JAMES GIBSON

ACKNOWLEDGMENTS

The publishers would like to thank the following for their kind permission to print the poems included in this anthology:

Danny Abse, for 'The Game' and 'A New Diary'; George Allen & Unwin Ltd, for 'Prose Poem towards a Definition of Itself' from *Little Johnny's Confession* and 'Interruption at the Opera House' from *Irrelevant Song*, by Brian Patten; Thomas Blackburn, for 'The Citizens' and 'Hospital for Defectives'; Jonathan Cape Ltd, for 'Good-bye to the Island' from *Collected Poems* and 'A Note from a Cello' from *Celebrations*, by William Plomer, and for 'Easter Poem' from *Fox on a Barn Door* and 'Swallows' from *The Night Bathers*, by Ted Walker; Chatto & Windus Ltd, for 'The Fossil Bird' from *The Scale of Things* and 'The Roman Wall' from *The World I See*, by Patric Dickinson, and for 'The Almond Tree' and 'Elm End' from *Root and Branch*, by Jon Stallworthy; The Trustees of the Estate of Richard Church, for 'Dis Alitur Visum' and 'A Recurrence'; J. M. Dent & Sons Ltd, for 'The Desert' and 'From Many a Mangled Truth' from *Collected Poems*, by Clifford Dyment, and for 'The Core of the Matter' from *White Shadows, Black Shadows* and 'Lost Dog' from *The Body Servant*, by James Kirkup; Faber & Faber Ltd, for 'Prologue at Sixty' and 'In Due Season' from *City Without Walls*, by W. H. Auden, for 'Asphodels: Chalcidice' and 'Orpheus' from *Collected Poems* by Lawrence Durrell, for 'The Wound' from *Fighting Terms* and 'Three' from *Moly*, by Thom Gunn, for 'Bogland' and 'The Peninsula' from *Door into the Dark*, by Seamus Heaney, for 'Second Glance at a Jaguar' and 'Full Moon and Little Frieda' from *Wodwo*, by Ted Hughes, for 'MCMXIV' and 'Send No Money' from *The Whitsun Weddings*, by Philip Larkin, for 'Villanelle for the Middle of the Way' from *The Golden Bird* and 'Choosing a Name' from *A Matter of Life and Death*, by Anne Ridler, and for 'Nocturne' from *Collected Poems 1928–1953* and 'One More New Botched Beginning' from *The Generous Days*, by Stephen Spender; Roy Fuller, for 'Poem' and 'Poem Out of Character'; Robert Gittings, for 'The Expert' and 'Sparrow'; Hamish Hamilton Ltd, for 'To the Daimon' and 'For the Bride' from *The Lost Country*, by Kathleen Raine; Rupert Hart-Davis, for 'Lore' and 'Those Others' from *Tares*, by R. S. Thomas; David Higham Associates Ltd, for 'Prinz Eugen' and 'A Short Life of Nevil Northey Burnard' from *Johnny Alleluia* (Rupert Hart-Davis), by Charles Causley, for 'Canso' and 'Plato and the Waters of the Flood' from *Selected Poems* (Oxford University Press), by John Heath-Stubbs, and for 'From a Boat at Coniston' from *The Pot Geranium*, by Norman Nicholson; David Holbrook, for 'Shall these Bones Live?' and 'Day with Infant'; Elizabeth Jennings, for 'For a Child Born Dead' and 'Fountain'; Laurie Lee, for 'Black Edge' and 'Bird'; Hope Leresche & Steele, for 'The Crusader' and 'George and the Dragonfly', by Roger McGough; Longman Group Ltd, for 'The Ass' and 'Angel Boley' from *The Scorpion and Other Poems*, by Stevie Smith; George MacBeth, for 'When I Am Dead' and 'Scissor-Man'; Macmillan (London and Basingstoke), for 'Common Sense' from *Sandgrains*

9

on a *Tray* and 'Elizabeth Pender's Dream of Friendship' from *Warriors Career*, by Alan Brownjohn, and for 'The Rock Pool' from *In Retreat and Other Poems* and 'The Ice Skaters' from *Coming Out Fighting*, by Philip Hobsbaum; John Murray (Publishers) Ltd, for 'Norfolk' and 'Remorse' from *Collected Poems*, by John Betjeman; Norman Nicholson, for 'Have You Been to London?'; Oxford University Press, for 'The Hermit to His Cat' and 'The Son', by Edward Lucie-Smith, for 'The Sadness of the Creatures' from *The Last of England*, by Peter Porter, for 'Arabic Script' and 'At Asqefar' from *The Stones of Emptiness*, by Anthony Thwaite, and for 'Swimming Chenango Lake' and 'Assassin' from *The Way of a World*, by Charles Tomlinson; A. D. Peters & Company, for 'New Approach Needed' and 'After Goliath' from *A Look Round the Estate* (Jonathan Cape Ltd), by Kingsley Amis, for 'Can You Remember?' and 'God's Time' from *Poems of Many Years* (Collins), by Edmund Blunden, and for extract from 'O Dreams, O Destinations' from *Word Over All* and 'On Not Saying Everything' from *From the Room* (Jonathan Cape Ltd), by C. Day Lewis; Ruth Pitter, for 'The Swifts'; Peter Porter, for 'The Great Poet Comes Here in Winter'; Punch Magazine, for 'Planting Mistletoe' by Ruth Pitter; Vernon Scannell, for 'A Case of Murder' and 'Walking Wounded'; A. P. Watt & Son, for 'Powers Unconfessed' and 'Solomon's Seal' from *Collected Poems 1968–1970*, by Robert Graves.

CONTENTS

11

15

DANNIE ABSE

I choose 'The Game' because this poem still surprises me when I read it. It seems to me to be cleverer than I am, more lyrical than I am, more pessimistic than I am. Perhaps to write about good and evil in terms of a football game seems extravagant. Yet many spectators act as if their team can do no wrong, as if their opponents are dirty, villainous, and can do no right. There is a ritualistic, primitive element in a soccer tournament with its committed supporters that allows the proposition, I think, that Good City can play Evil Town every Saturday of the football season.

So I don't feel that the football framework used as an allegorical device is an absurd one. And I have tried to be accurate. Professional football grounds all over the country do seem to have their quota of pigeons under the long tin roofs; small boys do swarm the field after the game is over; newsboys do greet the crowds leaving the match with headline voices announcing the latest disaster.

Throughout the poem I have chosen words taken from the common football vocabulary: 'passing', 'saved', 'transferred', 'heads up', etc. And of course I have used words ambiguously and punned unashamedly. Thus, when 'a hundred matches spark' this could refer either to the not unusual conversations about previous football matches, or could be a comment on those matches that light up pipes and cigarettes in the darkness of the stands. Lines such as 'A wing falls down when cherubs howl for blood', or 'and those who know the score just seem depressed' are but two further examples of the poem being clever. In short, not only was I writing about a game, in one sense I was also playing a game.

Perhaps what surprises me most about 'The Game', however, is its pessimism. After the 1914–1918 war, cripples were allowed, as a privilege and for their convenience, to sit around the touch-lines. By 1939 these cripples were fewer. Alas, after 1945 the cripples were back again in larger numbers, and it seems even now, in 1972, that the clean programmes trampled underfoot are not only the shiny football ones but the abstract political ones also.

Incidentally, 'The Game' was written in 1956 before floodlights had been installed, when a white ball was used in the middle of winter, in those murky, long-ago, Saturday afternoons of brass bands when we were young, or younger, or not yet born.

'A New Diary' I choose because I remember the pleasure it gave me in the writing of it. I was worried as I worked on the second stanza, for what had started off lightly had become King Lear-dark. I was afraid the tone of the poem had changed, ruining it, but the end came finally with a sudden rush and the sense, perhaps deluded sense, of 'bringing it off'. I think, I hope that: 'Oh my God,/Morwenna, Julie, don't forget me, Kate,' does return the poem to its original light tone and yet, at the same time, holds the dark centrality of it. For the conclusion has this deliberate ambiguity: after all, it can be read as if God is the who *'who, perhaps, is crossing out my name/now from some future diary', not just those girls with their pretty names.*

The Game

Follow the crowds to where the turnstiles click.
The terraces fill. *Hoompa*, blares the brassy band.
Saturday afternoon has come to Ninian Park
and, beyond the goalposts, in the Canton Stand
between black spaces, a hundred matches spark.

Waiting, we recall records, legendary scores:
Fred Keenor, Hardy, in a royal blue shirt.
The very names, sad as the old songs, open doors
before our time where someone else was hurt.
Now, like an injured beast, the great crowd roars.

The coin is spun. Here all is simplified
and we are partisan who cheer the Good,
hiss at passing Evil. Was Lucifer offside?
A wing falls down when cherubs howl for blood.
Demons have agents: the Referee is bribed.

The white ball smacked the crossbar. Satan rose
higher than the others in the smoked brown gloom
to sink on grass in a ballet dancer's pose.
Again, it seems, we hear a familiar tune
not quite identifiable. A distant whistle blows.

Memory of faded games, the discarded years;
talk of Aston Villa, Orient, and the Swans.
Half-time, the band played the same military airs
as when The Bluebirds once were champions.
Round touchlines, the same cripples in their chairs.

Mephistopheles had his joke. The honest team
dribbles ineffectually, no one can be blamed.
Infernal backs tackle, inside forwards scheme,
and if they foul us need we be ashamed?
Heads up! Oh for a Ted Drake, a Dixie Dean.

'Saved' or else, discontents, we are transferred
long decades back, like Faust must pay that fee.
The Night is early. Great phantoms in us stir
as coloured jerseys hover, move diagonally
on the damp turf, and our eidetic visions blur.

God sign our souls! Because the obscure Staff
of Hell rule this world, jugular fans guessed
the result halfway through the second half
and those who know the score just seem depressed.
Small boys swarm the field for an autograph.

Silent the Stadium. The crowds have all filed out.
Only the pigeons beneath the roofs remain.
The clean programmes are trampled underfoot,
and natural the dark, appropriate the rain,
whilst, under lamp-posts, threatening newsboys
    shout.

A New Diary

This clerk-work, this first January chore
of who's in, who's out. A list to think about
when absences seem to shout, Scandal! Outrage!
So turning to the blank, prefatory page
I transfer most of the names and phone tags
from last year's diary. True, Meadway, Speed-
    well,
Mountview, are computer-changed into
    numbers,
and already their pretty names begin to fade
like Morwenna, Julie, Don't-Forget-Me-Kate,
grassy, summer girls I once swore love to.
These, whispering others and time will date.

Cancelled, too, a couple someone else betrayed,
one man dying, another mind in rags.
And remembering them my clerk-work flags,
bitterly flags, for all lose, no one wins,
those in, those out, *this* at the heart of things.
So I stop, ask: whom should I commemorate,
and who, perhaps, is crossing out my name
now from some future diary? Oh my God,
Morwenna, Julie, don't forget me, Kate.

KINGSLEY AMIS

I suppose the most obvious reason why a poet prefers some of his poems to others is that he, by definition, is the only one who knows the more or less completely successful effort from the only partly successful. (If he has any sense, he doesn't let anybody see the really unsuccessful.) 'Success' here means, of course, not the achievement of a great poem, or even a good one, but success in the poet's own terms; in other words, having put into verse exactly what he meant to say in just the way he intended.

My poem, 'New Approach Needed', is one of my rare and lucky hits of this kind. Luck plays an undiscoverable part in these matters, a fact most poets will acknowledge, though they may give it more obviously mysterious names, like inspiration or the Muse. The poem came comparatively easily: no radical re-writing of the original draft proved necessary, merely a series of revisions.

Other, less 'successful' poems endear themselves to the poet because they have come to him with great difficulty. This was so with 'After Goliath', which changed its whole structure and poetic form several times in the writing. Like a model of St Paul's made out of matchsticks, it may not appeal to everybody, but I feel pleased with it because of all the work I put in.

∽∽∽∽∽

New Approach Needed

Should you revisit us,
Stay a little longer,
And get to know the place.
Experience hunger,
Madness, disease and war.
You heard about them, true,
The last time you came here;
It's different having them.
And what about a go
At love, marriage, children?
All good, but bringing some
Risk of remorse and pain
And fear of an odd sort:
A sort one should, again,
Feel, not just hear about,
To be qualified as
A human-race expert.
On local life, we trust
The resident witness
Not the royal tourist.

People have suffered worse
And more durable wrongs
Than you did on that cross
(I know—you won't get me
Up on one of those things),
Without sure prospect of
Ascending good as new
On the third day, without
'I die, but man shall live'
As a nice cheering thought.

So, next time, come off it,
And get some service in,
Jack, long before you start

Laying down the old law:
If you still want to then.
Tell your dad that from me.

After Goliath

What shall be done to the man
that killeth this Philistine?

I Sam. xvii, 27

The first shot out of that sling
Was enough to finish the thing:
The champion laid out cold
Before half the programmes were sold.
And then, what howls of dismay
From his fans in their dense array:
From aldermen, adjutants, aunts,
Administrators of grants,
Assurance-men, auctioneers,
Advisers about careers,
And advertisers, of course,
Plus the obvious b——s in force:
The whole reprehensible throng
Ten times an alphabet strong.
But such an auspicious debut
Was a little too good to be true,
Our victor sensed; the applause
From those who supported his cause
Sounded shrill and excessive now,
And who were they, anyhow?
Academics, actors who lecture,
Apostles of architecture,
Ancient-gods-of-the-abdomen men,
Angst-pushers, adherents of Zen,
Alastors, Austenites, A-test

Abolishers—even the straightest
Of issues look pretty oblique
When a movement turns into a clique,
The conqueror mused, as he stopped
By the sword his opponent had dropped:
Trophy, or means of attack
On the rapturous crowd at his back?
He shrugged and left it, resigned
To a new battle, fought in the mind,
For faith that his quarrel was just,
That the right man lay in the dust.

W. H. AUDEN

Every poet, I think, complains about the laziness of anthologists, who simply copy each other. Also no poet wants to hear again about his old war-horses. They may be good poems but he is bored by the thought of them.

As regards my own work, I have some unfavourites but no favourites. Naturally, I am more interested in what I have been writing fairly recently than in the distant past. The two I pick are both in City without Walls.

The first, 'In Due Season', I choose because it is the only English poem since Campion written in accentual asclepiads; the second, 'Prologue at Sixty', because I think the alliterative metre is not badly handled.

∽∾∽∾∽∾

In Due Season

Spring-time, Summer and Fall: days to behold a world
Antecedent to our knowing, where flowers think
Theirs concretely in scent-colours and beasts, the same
Age all over, pursue dumb horizontal lives
On one level of conduct and so cannot be
Secretary to man's plot to become divine.

Lodged in all is a set metronome: thus, in May
Bird-babes still in the egg click to each other *Hatch!*;
June-struck cuckoos go off-pitch; when obese July

26

Turns earth's heating up, unknotting their poisoned
   ropes,
Vipers move into play; warned by October's nip,
Younger leaves to the old give the releasing draught.

Winter, though, has the right tense for a look indoors
At ourselves, and with First Names to sit face-to-face,
Time for reading of thoughts, time for the trying-out
Of new metres and new recipes, proper time
To reflect on events noted in warmer months
Till, transmuted they take part in a human tale.

There, responding to our cry for intelligence,
Nature's mask is relaxed into a mobile grin,
Stones, old shoes, come alive, born sacramental signs,
Nod to us in the First Person of mysteries
They know nothing about, bearing a message from
The invisible sole Source of specific things.

Prologue at Sixty

(for Friedrich Heer)

Dark-green upon distant heights
the stationary flocks foresters tend,
blonde and fertile the fields below them:
browing a hog-back, an oak stands
post-alone, light-demanding.

Easier to hear, harder to see,
limbed lives, locomotive,
automatic and irritable,
social or solitary, seek their foods,
mates and territories while their time lasts.

Radial republics, rooted to spots,
bilateral monarchies, moving frankly,
stoic by sort and self-policing,
enjoy their rites, their realms of data,
live well by the Law of their Flesh.

All but the youngest of the yawning mammals,
Name-Giver, Ghost-Fearer,
maker of wars and wise-cracks,
a rum creature, in a crisis always,
the anxious species to which I belong,

whom chance and my own choice have arrived
to bide here yearly from bud-haze
to leaf-blush, dislodged from elsewhere,
by blood barbarian, in bias of view
a Son of the North, outside the *limes*.

Rapacious pirates my people were,
crude and cruel, but not calculating,
never marched in step nor made straight roads,
nor sank like senators to a slave's taste
for grandiose buildings and gladiators.

But the Gospel reached the unroman lands.
I can translate what onion-towers
of five parish churches preach in Baroque:
to make One, there must be Two,
Love is substantial, all Luck is good,

Flesh must fall through fated time
from birth to death, both unwilled,
but Spirit may climb counterwise
from a death, in faith freely chosen,
to resurrection, a re-beginning.

And the Greek Code got to us also:
a Mind of Honour must acknowledge

the happy eachness of all things,
distinguish even from odd numbers,
and bear witness to what-is-the-case.

East, West, on the Autobahn
motorists whoosh, on the Main Line
a far-sighted express will snake by,
through a gap granted by grace of nature:
still today, as in the Stone Age,

our sandy vale is a valued passage.
Alluvial flats, flooded often,
lands of outwash, lie to the North,
to the South litters of limestone alps
embarrass the progress of path-seekers.

Their thoughts upon ski-slope or theatre-
        opening,
few who pass us pay attention
to our squandered hamlets where at harvest
        time
chugging tractors, child-driven,
shamble away down sheltered lanes.

Quiet now but acquainted too
with unwelcome visitors, violation,
scare and scream, the scathe of battle:
Turks have been here, Boney's legions,
Germans, Russians, and no joy they brought.

Though the absence of hedge-rows is odd to me
(no Whig landlord, the landscape vaunts,
ever empired on Austrian ground),
this unenglish tract after ten years
into my love has looked itself,

added its names to my numinous map
of the *Solihull* gas-works, gazed at in awe

by a bronchial boy, the *Blue John Mine*,
the *Festiniog* railway, the *Rhayader* dams,
Cross Fell, Keld and *Cauldron Snout,*

of sites made sacred by something read there,
a lunch, a good lay, or sheer lightness of heart,
the *Fürbringer* and the *Friedrich Strasse,*
Isafjördur, Epomeo,
Poprad, Basel, Bar-le-Duc,

of more modern holies, *Middagh Street,*
Carnegie Hall and the *Con-Ed* stacks
on *First Avenue*. Who am I now?
An American? No, a New Yorker,
who opens his *Times* at the obit page,

whose dream images date him already,
awake among lasers, electric brains,
do-it-yourself sex manuals,
bugged phones, sophisticated
weapon-systems and sick jokes.

Already a helpless orbited dog
has blinked at our sorry conceited O,
where many are famished, few look good,
and my day turned out torturers
who read *Rilke* in their rest periods.

Now the Cosmocrats are crashed through time-
        zones
in jumbo jets to a Joint Conference:
nor sheep nor shit have our shepherds had,
and treaties are signed (with secret clauses)
by Heads who are not all there.

Can Sixty make sense to Sixteen-Plus?
What has my camp in common with theirs,
with buttons and beards and Be-Ins?

Much, I hope. In *Acts* it is written
Taste was no problem at Pentecost.

To speak is human because human to listen,
beyond hope, for an Eighth Day,
when the creatured Image shall become the
    Likeness:
Giver-of-Life, translate for me
till I accomplish my corpse at last.

JOHN BETJEMAN

Some years ago I was visiting East Anglia when I suddenly found myself in the train going past the very place I'd spent many weeks in when I was ten years old. I remembered those early days when everything seemed so exciting—and so full of hope. I've tried to express in my poem, 'Norfolk', the feeling of those days compared with the feeling of guilt one has all the time now that one is older, the feeling that one has besmirched the wonderful opportunities that one has had.

My second poem, 'Remorse', comes straight from the heart. It is about a death-bed scene at which I was present.

∽∽∽∽∽

Norfolk

How did the Devil come? When first attack?
　　These Norfolk lanes recall lost innocence,
The years fall off and find me walking back
　　Dragging a stick along the wooden fence
Down this same path, where, forty years ago,
My father strolled behind me, calm and slow.

I used to fill my hands with sorrel seeds
　　And shower him with them from the tops of stiles,
I used to butt my head into his tweeds
　　To make him hurry down those languorous miles
Of ash and alder-shaded lanes, till here
Our moorings and the masthead would appear.

There after supper lit by lantern light
  Warm in the cabin I could lie secure
And hear against the polished sides at night
  The lap lap lapping of the weedy Bure,
A whispering and watery Norfolk sound
Telling of all the moonlit reeds around.

How did the Devil come? When first attack?
  The church is just the same though now I know
Fowler of Louth restored it. Time, bring back
  The rapturous ignorance of long ago,
The peace, before the dreadful daylight starts,
Of unkept promises and broken hearts.

Remorse

The lungs draw in the air and rattle it out again;
  The eyes revolve in their sockets and upwards stare;
No more worry and waiting and troublesome doubt
    again—
  She whom I loved and left is no longer there.

The nurse puts down her knitting and walks across
    to her,
  With quick professional eye she surveys the dead.
Just one patient the less and little the loss to her,
  Distantly tender she settles the shrunken head.

Protestant claims and Catholic, the wrong and the
    right of them,
  Unimportant they seem in the face of death—
But my neglect and unkindness—to lose the sight of
    them
  I would listen even again to that labouring breath.

THOMAS BLACKBURN

'The Citizens'. Myths and good fairy stories tell us through their images about states of mind and the wanderings and dangers of the soul on its journey between life and death. We no longer believe literally in vampires and were-wolves but for all that the savage unpredictable energies which myths used to symbolize are still with us as inhabitants of the depths of the human psyche. In this poem I have tried to suggest that although we no longer have a literal belief in the creatures of myth, they are still with us. Indeed, if we do not learn to understand ourselves, we may well be destroyed by our own unacknowledged violence.

'Hospital for Defectives'. I watched some mental defectives working in a turnip field near a hospital. Some of them pulled and pushed a cart and one had the job of catching the turnips and placing them in the cart after the warder had slashed off the top leaves with a large knife. Something was tickling his nose and he kept muffing his catches. After a while the warder lost his patience and slapped the man three times across the mouth. The defective did not wince or cry out—he just stood still in the pouring rain, his white face lifted upward. I use the term 'Lord of the Images' because like 'love' the word 'God' has been so manhandled. What power is it that can make something as beautiful as an eyelid and as terrible as a hydrocephalic idiot? The nearest we can get to an answer is by asking the question as accurately as possible.

∞∞∞∞∞

The Citizens

After the marsh was drained and its vast monsters
Had gasped their lives out in the well-rinsed air,
Our city corporation cleaned the fosse up
And charged us sixpence to see Grendell's lair.
We thought that with the great Panjandrum banished
An era of sweet dreams was sure to start;
But gracious no; only his cave has vanished:
Don't look now, but he's walking in your heart.

After Sir Hercules had combed the mountains
And killed the Nemean lion, our woods were bare.
On feast days now we can go out to picnic
And if it rains take shelter in its lair:
The pebbles and the moss are quite enchanting.
I think I hear the ancient roaring start.
What's that you say? I said the ancient roaring,
Excuse me but it's coming from your heart.

Upon our museum shelves we keep the omens
That after school before they go to bed
Children may see some curious time-worn bauble,
A pickled toad, a stone, a Gorgon's head.
Why do they cry in sleep, the silly children,
Of birds that speak, of snakes that hiss and dart
Upon a woman's scalp? Put them to silence.
You cannot stop the language of the heart.

In days gone by the warriors would sit feasting,
Then freeze to silence at the slow footfall
Of Grendell's furious dam who rocked the postern,
Then strode through snapping beams into the hall.
That monster comes no more by field or river,
But still our dwelling place is torn apart
By human hands—like mine—our children ravaged:
Oh, hide me from the fury of the heart.

Hospital for Defectives

By your unnumbered charities
A miracle disclose,
Lord of the Images, whose love
The eyelid and the rose
Takes for a language, and today
Tell to me what is said
By these men in a turnip field
And their unleavened bread.

For all things seem to figure out
The stirrings of your heart,
And two men pick the turnips up
And two men pull the cart;
And yet between the four of them
No word is ever said
Because the yeast was not put in
Which makes the human bread.
But three men stare on vacancy
And one man strokes his knees;
What is the meaning to be found
In such dark vowels as these?

Lord of the Images, whose love
The eyelid and the rose
Takes for a metaphor, today
Beneath the warder's blows,
The unleavened man did not cry out
Or turn his face away;
Through such men in a turnip field
What is it that you say?

EDMUND BLUNDEN

*Both the poems I choose are personal poems—one of War
and one of Peace. My experiences in the First World War
have haunted me all my life and for many days I have,
it seemed, lived in that world rather than this.*

*'God's Time', written during the Second World War,
is based on an actual walk, and a real sense of Peace
throwing all else out.*

∞∞∞∞∞

'Can You Remember?'

Yes, I still remember
    The whole thing in a way;
Edge and exactitude
    Depend on the day.

Of all that prodigious scene
    There seems scanty loss,
Though mists mainly float and screen
    Canal, spire and fosse;

Though commonly I fail to name
    That once obvious Hill,
And where we went and whence we came
    To be killed, or kill.

Those mists are spiritual
And luminous obscure,
Evolved of countless circumstance
Of which I am sure;

Of which, at the instance
Of sound, smell, change and stir,
New-old shapes for ever
Intensely recur.

And some are sparkling, laughing, singing,
Young, heroic, mild;
And some incurable, twisted,
Shrieking, dumb, defiled.

God's Time

A gentler heaven steals over the hour,
And at its pace I go
And scan green things that grow
Beneath old hedge and ivy-bower.
Most gracious falls the silent hour.

Through the shut sky an eye of blue
Twinkles upon the soul,
Even as these weeds unroll
Their leaves aspiring, choice and new;
Their greenness blesses, and that blue.

The round leaf, shield leaf, patterned spray
All shine like love's first tears,
And though no primrose peers,
Nor aconites, nor windflowers play,
I have their message through leaf and spray.

This may not be the hour I supposed
    When from the house I came
    Informed of a world aflame;
That will have been an era closed,
Though endless as I then supposed.

O green leaves born in winter's heart,
    White ghosts of flowers to be,
    Come here so quietly,
And blossoming heaven's blue counterpart,
—I have lost my way, and found my heart.

ALAN BROWNJOHN

'*Common Sense*'. *The editor of an avant-garde magazine asked me to send him a poem. I had no poems, and no ideas for poems—until I opened, by accident, an old arithmetic book which belonged to my grandfather. Turning over the pages, I was struck by the examples used in the various arithmetical problems: they seemed to me to reflect in an amusing—or even an alarming—way the period in which the sums were devised. They seemed to say something very revealing about the kind of world into which the young children tackling the sums were growing up. Accordingly, I took six of the sums, re-arranged them just a little, and set them out in verses of poetry to make a satirical poem about the world of 1917 (the last verse is taken from the introduction to the book). This is what is called, I suppose, a 'found' poem rather than a written one. Because the things described in the sums may have seemed 'common sense' to people in 1917 (if not today), and because the book was called a* Common Sense Arithmetic, *I called the poem simply 'Common Sense'.*

'*Elizabeth Pender's Dream of Friendship*'. *I had been writing a number of poems which included invented names—invented rather in the way a novelist would invent them, though not often a poet. I found that these invented characters began to have attitudes towards, and relation-ships with, one another—and thoughts of their own. Elizabeth Pender occurs in two or three other poems, and in this one she has a dream which reflects the fears she has about the loyalty and goodwill of her friends. In the course of this nightmare, she is deserted by all her truest friends in a situation of mystery, horror and insecurity, and left in a lonely situation which seems to have no solution. In effect, the poem is a kind of short story, and is loosely based on a dream which a friend actually had— but a lot of other things, including Elizabeth Pender's name, have been invented, and the nightmare described is a long way from the dream experience which inspired it.*

Common Sense

An agricultural labourer, who has
A wife and four children, receives 20*s* a week.
¾ buys food, and the members of the family
Have three meals a day.
How much is that per person per meal?
   —*From Pitman's Common Sense Arithmetic, 1917*

A gardener, paid 24*s* a week, is
Fined 1/3 if he comes to work late.
At the end of 26 weeks, he receives
£30. 5. 3. How
Often was he late?
   —*From Pitman's Common Sense Arithmetic, 1917*

A milk dealer buys milk at 3*d* a quart. He
Dilutes it with 3% water and sells
124 gallons of the mixture at
4*d* per quart. How much of his profit is made by
Adulterating the milk?
   —*From Pitman's Common Sense Arithmetic, 1917*

The table printed below gives the number
Of paupers in the United Kingdom, and
The total cost of poor relief.

Find the average number
Of paupers per ten thousand people.
            —*From Pitman's Common Sense Arithmetic, 1917*

An army had to march to the relief of
A besieged town, 500 miles away, which
Had telegraphed that it could hold out for 18 days.
The army made forced marches at the rate of 18
Miles a day. Would it be there in time?
            —*From Pitman's Common Sense Arithmetic, 1917*

Out of an army of 28,000 men,
15% were
Killed, 25% were
Wounded. Calculate
How many men there were left to fight.
            —*From Pitman's Common Sense Arithmetic, 1917*

These sums are offered to
That host of young people in our Elementary Schools,
        who
Are so ardently desirous of setting
Foot upon the first rung of the
Educational ladder. . . .
            —*From Pitman's Common Sense Arithmetic, 1917*

Elizabeth Pender's Dream of Friendship

        When all these men and
        women came, in
        the sunlight, to that
              tower they
        found it
        was embedded

in the earth. And
to get inside, you
crossed over this
iron bridge, to meet
spiralling
　　　downward
steps;
which they did,
and proceeded down
-stairs to a room
with only a
white
telephone in it and one
window looking out at hills
holding a sea back.
And when the
telephone immediately
　　　rang,
a voice told them
don't
go, whatever
else you do, out
by the middle stair
-case door if the
　　　horse
is standing in the field with
tresses of blood-wet
silk at its mouth.
How then to
　　　get away,
all these lovers and friends,
because when
they
　　　opened that door,
they saw, in blank fright
the enormous horse
waiting
　　　and looking

43

and waiting,
and they must not, could
not go out. Still,
at the top of the spiral of
steps, it was a
hundred fears worse:
a darkening
field of
broken
inscribed
    graves, which moved
and edged to
-wards them,
and utterly white
funerary
    statues,
embracing.
At that top door, they
held one
another, tightly, but
    who,
when they looked,
exactly
    who
were their friends?
Because one by
one, everyone
    not
thoroughly true to her,
or to himself,
or to herself
was irrevocably
    dissolving,
and it was starting to
be, very suddenly,
    night.
It was so
    black now, they

couldn't even make out
which of each other's
faces
were still
truly
        there,
in which fear
she, and they, tried
hard (it was so
hard) to breathe and tried
to speak and tried to
think how possible in any
-thing like this,
        any
-thing like dawn
actually

was.

CHARLES CAUSLEY

'Prinz Eugen' is concerned with the fatal, but necessary, flaw in what might otherwise appear to be perfect beauty (of character, intellect, personality, etc.)—a theme that has always attracted me. This flaw is the essential quality that humanizes, brings nearer, what might else seem remote, divine, totally unapproachable.

'A Short Life of Nevil Northey Burnard' is about Burnard, born the son of a stone-mason in a remote village on Bodmin Moor in Cornwall, who became one of the most celebrated sculptors of Victorian times. On the death of a favourite child, and at the height of his fame, he abandoned wife, home, commissions, the whole of London and its associations, and returned to Cornwall and the scenes of his childhood as a common tramp. His story has never been fully documented or told; and the enigma of his personality has fascinated me for many years.

∞∞∞∞∞

Prinz Eugen

Prinz Eugen walked on the castle wall,
His eye was long and his leg was tall.
'Do you not fear, Prince,' I said, 'you will fall?'
Never, he answered. *Never at all.*

'Gold is your head and gold your groin,
Your nose is as neat as a Roman coin.
The spin of your skin has never a join!'

Look, said the Prince, *at my lip and my loin.*
Look at the silver that springs from my thumb,
Look for the brown blood that never will come.
Teach my beached heart the soft speech of the drum,
Feather with words the straw birds as they hum.
On my cold castle the strict sea knocks,
Butters his blade on the rim of the rocks.
Do you not hear how his ticking tongue mocks,
Slits every second and keel-hauls the clocks?

'Prince, but your gilt-edged eyebrow curls,
You stop your sentences up with pearls.
What will you do with all the girls
When love his lamp-black flag unfurls?
And Prince, your platinum fingers play
Over the maps and far away.
Are you not lord of all you survey?'
Then I am blind, I heard him say.

'Bright is your bed as the sailing shore,
Its posters up to the ceiling soar.
The servants stand at your dazzling door
To strip your senses to the core.
White is the light at your driven head,
Your body of corn stands straight as bread.
Why is your beating breast unfed?
Is it because you are dead, are dead?'

Envy me not this cloth of clay
That dries to dust all through the day.
Hurtle your heart on the pouring bay,
Answered Prinz Eugen, and limped away.

A Short Life of Nevil Northey Burnard

Cornish Sculptor 1818–1878

Here lived Burnard who with his finger's bone
Broke syllables of light from the moorstone,
Spat on the genesis of dust and clay,
Rubbed with sure hands the blinded eyes of day,
And through the seasons of the talking sun
Walked, calm as God, the fields of Altarnun.

Here, where St. Nonna with a holy reed
Hit the bare granite, made the waters bleed,
Madmen swam to their wits in her clear well,
Young Burnard fasted, watched, learned how to tell
Stone beads under the stream, and at its knock
Quietly lifted out his prize of rock.

As Michelangelo by stone possessed
Sucked the green marble from his mother's breast
So Burnard, at his shoulder the earth's weight,
Received on his child's tongue wafers of slate
And when he heard his granite hour strike
Murdered Christ's hangman with a mason's spike.

The village sprawled white as a marriage bed,
Gulls from the north coast stumbled overhead
As Burnard, standing in the church-yard hay,
Leaned on the stiff light, hacked childhood away,
On the tomb slabs watched bugler, saint, dove,
Under his beating fists grow big with love.

The boy with the Laocoön's snake crown
Caught with a six-inch nail the stinking town.
He turned, as Midas, men to stone, then gold.
Forgot, he said, what it was to be cold.
Birds rang like coins. He spread his fingers wide.
Wider the gulfs of love as his child died.

Packing only his heart, a half-hewn stone,
He left house, clothes, goods, blundered off alone:
London to Cornwall and the spinning moor,
Slept in stacks, hedges, barns, retraced the spoor
Of innocence; through the lost shallows walked,
Of his dead child, they say, for ever talked.

At last, the dragged November sun on high,
Burnard lay in a mumpers' inn to die.
At Redruth Workhouse, with the stripped, insane,
Banged on death's door and did not bang in vain;
Rocked in a gig to sleep in pauper's clay
Where three more warmed his side till judgement
        day.

No mourner stood to tuck him in God's bed,
Only the coffin-pusher. Overhead,
The fishing rooks unravelling the hour,
Two men, a boy, restored Camborne Church tower.
'This box,' the clerk said, 'holds your man in place.'
'We come,' they said, 'to smooth dirt from his face.'

No cross marks the spot where he first saw day.
Time with a knife wears the dull flesh away,
Peels the soft skin of blocks cut on the green
Signed by a boy, 'Burnard. Sculptor. Thirteen'.
Slowly the land shakes as the ocean's gun
Sounds over Cornwall. He stares from the sun.

The torn tramp, rough with talents, walks the park.
Children have swift stones ready. Men, dogs, bark.

The light falls on the bay, the cold sea leaks,
The slate face flushes, opens its lips, speaks.
In from the moor the pointing shadows flock,
Finger, beneath the river, the pure rock.

RICHARD CHURCH

Both the poems I have chosen have been written only recently. Both are characteristic of an old man's mood, tending to be introspective but resigned, and unconsciously detaching himself from his personal anchorage in this world, rather in the manner of Landor's quatrain in farewell, that ended,

> I warmed both hands before the fire of life;
> It sinks, and I am ready to depart.

I notice this in the later works of Yeats, Hardy and Masefield.

∽∽∽∽∽

Dis Alitur Visum

Do not believe the illusion. We have seen
Growth and decay of centuries, imposed upon
Our life-load. Is that not enough to carry,
Tottering to senility and the grave?
Show some respect at least, if you are young
And therefore quite incapable of pity.
Those who grow old, although they appear
    shrunken,
Maintain unwithered ecstasies of love,
Eternal moments by an inland lake
Watching the sunset waters with a lover

51

Long since vanished, yet remembered still,
Ever elusive, ever disappearing,
A mockery of some divine ascension
Told of in dead religions, when mankind
Believed in a hereafter, to repair
This dreadful cheat of our mortality,
With love betrayed by what it feeds upon,
As those lake waters counterfeit the stars.

A Recurrence

All Easter Saturday a high wind blew,
It was no normal wind, to come and go
As Nature breathes above the melted snow
And prophesies of flowers, as if it knew
Nothing but gentleness, and morning dew.
This other was persistent in its flow,
I felt an angry accusation glow
Invincible but fiery as it grew
Fiercer and fiercer from the Middle East
Till Christian Europe cowered, and Britain
    shrank
Sullen and guilty as a stricken beast
Beneath this punishment, whose sound of
    doom
Proclaimed accusing angels, rank on rank,
Rolling the stone, God-bidden, from a
    Tomb.

PATRIC DICKINSON

I have collected fossils since I was eight. Whether they are urchins, shells, the vertebrae of an ichthyosaurus (my greatest find), ammonites—I hold their still stone in my hand and feel the millions of years of its livingness and changeability. I have made 'The Fossil Bird' into the fantasy of one of these creatures suddenly coming alive and mocking me—Man—for failing to change. So in 'The Roman Wall' I'm trying to show how fluid I feel history is. (And the road has the image of vertebrae!) I believe also that it is well to be true; *the poor Astures* must *have shivered; all Roman armies got standard 'Samian Ware' from three great potteries in Gaul. These two poems really say the same thing in quite different ways. To me the world is a living place and there is so much to feel and to see and to love and to discover.*

> Often when I'm alone in a wild place
> If I find a stone I move it. . . .

Perhaps human beings need sometimes to be moved like this if they are going to enjoy to the full the world they live in.

∽∽∽∽∽

The Fossil Bird

The fossil bird spoke from the stone:
'I'm bored. Do they never change?
Egg by egg, song by song,
All by rote and never a note wrong—
It wasn't like that when I was young,'
Said the fossil bird.

I picked him up, I hurled him high
And 'Fly, then!' in human pride I mocked.
He flew. My heart went stone in my breast.
'Alas, I was looking for a nest,
And you're no better than the rest,'
Said the fossil bird.

Now like Poe's raven, he sticks to my shoulder.
I grow old, I grow older, more craven, more
    indifferent
To the human situation—*Oh why do you wait
Croaking I'm bored, I'm bored till I hate you?*
'You may turn into something yet,'
Said the fossil bird.

The Roman Wall

The cars speed up and down. Under the surface lie
Foundations of the Wall, like the fossil vertebrae
Of an extinct animal. The cars speed up and down,
Their radios lilt and lull, till from his blind watch-tower
A reader gives them news, half-heeded and half-heard
Between Wallsend and Carlisle, of contending worlds to
    choose,

Of the molten core of Power on whose thin crust they
    ride.
Above and Roman-straight is a bomber's vapour-trail,
Below at the gate of Cilurnum the Emperor's post from
    Rome.

Here the Astures watched shivering in the rain,
Conquered auxiliaries, cavalrymen from Spain,
But eating and drinking from mass-produced Samian-
    ware,
Pretending to like baths, and generally behaving
In a low Roman fashion, defending a civilisation
Few would enjoy by saving and fewer understand;
Yet trained to fight to the death for their fostermother-
    land
As if they could really care for the system of its Law—
And now the Emperor's word: the order to withdraw.

In their ruined bath-house I try to re-animate the scene,
To hear the steamy shouts of the glistening naked men,
Till the last man is out, and dressed in his time again;
The stoker draws the fires, the water soon goes cold.
Naked to silence here by the long-broken bounds
Of the Pax Romana I shiver and watch the sky.
Where they laid their uniforms in lockers of neat stone
Long folded echoes lie, but I dare not put them on
Lest they clothe me with a voice: *Suppose our language
    die?*

The cars speed up and down the temporal surfaces,
The vapour-trail has turned to innocent-looking cloud;
Between Wallsend and Carlisle there is no news today.
The lulling music drowns the order to withdraw,
Half-heeded and half-heard, it drowns the living word
That condemns the innocent by process of natural Law.
Yesterday they went with underhopes of home
And mostly glad to go—how impotent to save
A Rome already burned perhaps their leaders know.

LAWRENCE DURRELL

One cannot really say much about why one poem seems to come off better than another: and people seem never to agree as to the why and wherefore. 'Asphodels: Chalcidice' and 'Orpheus' seem okay to me. They capture and fix moods and feelings which were personally very close to me when I wrote them.

∽∽∽∽∽

Asphodels: Chalcidice

'No one will ever pick them, I think,
The ugly off-white clusters: all the grace
Lies in the name of death named.
Are they a true certificate for death?'
        'I wonder.'

'You might say that once the sages,
Death being identified, forgave it language:
Called it "asphodel", as who should say
The synonym for scentless, colourless,
        Solitary,

Rock-loving . . .' 'Memory is all of these.'
'Yes, they asserted the discipline of memory,
Which admits of no relapse in its
Consignment, does not keep forever.'
        'Nor does death.'

'You mean our dying?' 'No, but when one is
Alone, neither happy nor unhappy, in
The deepest ache of reason where this love
Becomes a malefactor, clinging so,
      You surely know—'

'Death's stock will stand no panic,
Be beautiful in jars or on a coffin,
Exonerate the flesh when it has turned
Or mock the enigma with an epitaph
      It never earned.'

'These quite precisely guard ironic truth,
And you may work your way through every
Modulation of the rose, to fill your jars
With pretty writing-stuff: but for death—'
      'Truly, always give us

These comfortless, convincing, even, yes,
A little mocking, Grecian asphodels.'

Orpheus

Orpheus, beloved famulus,
Known to us in a dark congeries
Of intimations from the dead:
Encamping among our verses—
Harp-beats of a sea-bird's wings—
Do you contend in us, though now
A memory only, the smashed lyre
Washed up entangled in your hair,
But sounding still as here,
O monarch of all initiates and
The dancer's only peer?

In the fecund silences of the
Painter, or the poet's wrestling
With choice you steer like
A great albatross, spread white
On the earth-margins the sailing
Snow-wings in the world's afterlight:
Mentor of all these paper ships
Cockled from fancy on a tide
Made navigable only by your skill
Which in some few approves
A paper recreation of lost loves.

CLIFFORD DYMENT

I have chosen these two poems because each has something to say about an anxiety of our time.

'The Desert'. A friend once suggested to me that this poem should be called 'The Bomb'. That is a possible title, yes: but it's too specific, narrows the theme too much—for the poem isn't only about atomic devastation. It came to me in a dream and describes a vision of desolation caused by global nuclear war, or by soil erosion, or by toxic chemicals in agriculture, or by pollution of air and water, or by some other agency of man's destructive impulse. But the poem isn't entirely negative: it affirms man's creativity even in the midst of ruin.

'From Many a Mangled Truth a War Is Won'. Many years ago I accepted Aldous Huxley's premise that 'means determine ends'—that good ends can't be attained by bad means. But time has made me increasingly uncertain of this proposition. A lie can create faith and so achieve a seeming miracle; violent demonstrations can get wrongs put right; wars can secure benefits. There is injustice in authoritarian countries—but so there is in democracies. Fascist regimes oppress minorities—but so do Communist ones. What is bad? What is good? How can we say? Until the ultimate enlightenment (if any) in our imperfect state we see as in a glass, darkly, and all we can do is use imperfections to seek perfection out.

The Desert

Beside a dune high as a tree
  But spreading no tree's shade
A man and boy sat silently
  Working at their trade.

A heap of bones lay on the sand
  Like barkless staves of wood;
And near it lay a second heap
  Polished with thickening blood.

One bone, two bones, three bones were
  Chosen by the man
Who made of them a heart's shape, wide
  As his two hands would span.

The man and boy sat hour by hour
  Calmly, coolly, dumb,
Feeling the scarlet heat as though
  Their blackened skins were numb.

A third heap soon rose at their side
  Like boughs laid for a pyre:
The boy's hand went to it and took
  From many lyres one lyre.

It was a lyre in shape, but where
  The stream of music springs
The lyre was nought, a mouth crying
  Wordlessly for strings.

The boy reached to the heap that shone
  Untouched on the sand
And from its bloody muteness drew
  A bloody speaking hand.

He fixed the voice in place, then more,
And soon the lyre was strung—
A frame made of three human bones,
Each string a human tongue.

The old man took the brilliant lyre
And struck its cords of red;
The boy rapt by his side stood up
As a snake rears up its head

And with no smile and with no sigh
Moved to the lyre's sounds
In a world all dust save for a man,
A dancer, and three mounds.

'From Many a Mangled Truth a War Is Won'

From many a mangled truth a war is won
And who am I to oppose
War and the lie and the pose
Asserting a lie is good if a war be won?

From many a mangled truth a war is won
And many a truth has died
That has lived undenied
For always there must be loss that a war
be won.

From many a mangled truth a war is won
And when no truth is pure
Who of us can be sure
Of lie and truth and war when the war is
won?

ROY FULLER

'Poem' was published in New Verse *in December 1934. For an unknown provincial young man, to achieve publication in a first-class avant-garde magazine (New Verse was the organ of the Auden-inspired new poetry of the time) came as an excitement and encouragement scarcely to be experienced again. (I should add that the poem has never since been reprinted!) 'Poem Out of Character' was written in the 1950s. As its title indicates, it marked a change of manner that rarely happens in a poet's work. Quite suddenly, in my forties, I realized that greater themes, a higher style, might be within my scope.*

∽∽∽∽∽

Poem

In a normal rainfall the channel was adequate,
but all that summer, under dripping trees,
I waited watching pyrotechnics on macadam.
The bosom of the wounded land was swollen
and gaped revealing the red clay.
Subterranean courses percolated, causing
litigation among former neighbours.
In the roaring gutters the leaves became sodden
like bread in a sink, and exercised, perhaps,
    control.
From the ground coiled unknown roots,
fantastic and demanding sustenance.
The whole territory was darkened under veils.

Along lines of communication to my room
the crystal beads ran fast and runnelled
from porcelain pots, boring the noisy gravel.
Under hot sheets I listened
hoping yet not hoping the channel was adequate,
and in the black morning after brief slumber,
waking startled to the sound of it and a thundery
sky.

Poem Out of Character

Rapidly moving from the end
To the middle of anthologies,
The poet starts to comprehend
The styles that never can be his.

The dreams of tremendous statements fade,
Inchoate still the passionate rhymes
Of men, the novel verse form made
To satirize and warn the times.

And yet at moments, as in sleep,
Beyond his book float images—
Those four great planets swathed in deep
Ammoniac and methane seas.

He walks the ruined autumn scene—
The trees a landscape painter's brown,
And through the foreground rags, serene
The faded sky, palladian town.

Or thinks of man, his single young,
The failure of the specialized,
Successful type; the curious, long
Years before earth was dramatized:

The West Wind Drift, that monstrous belt
Of sea below the planet's waist:
The twenty-one world cultures felt
Like fathers, doomed to be defaced.

Yes, these vast intimations rise
And still I merely find the words
For symbols of a comic size—
Ambiguous cats and sweets and birds.

Viewed through such tiny apertures
The age presents a leaf, a hair,
An inch of skin; while what enures,
In truth, behind the barrier,

Weltering in blood, enormous joys
Lighting their faces, is a frieze
Of giantesses, gods and boys;
And lions and inhuman trees.

ROBERT GITTINGS

Many of my poems begin by recording a single isolated personal experience. The experience can be something I have read; 'The Expert' was written after reading a book about the Treblinka extermination camp. After setting down the experience exactly, I find it often seems to broaden and have a more general meaning, one I had not quite anticipated when I first tried to write. This seems to be the pattern of a good many of my shorter poems.

∞∞∞∞∞

The Expert

A bottleneck existed at Camp Five.
The dead were dying quicker than they should.
The burning bodies doused the kindling wood.
All waited for the expert to arrive.

He came with briefcase, a neat blueprint man.
He had the theory and he knew the fact.
The fault was how the bodies had been stacked.
His demonstration instantly began.

The bodies must be used to burn each other.
The old, the fat, the female were the best:
The base of these, a pyramid the rest—
The sons were fuelled by their sulphurous
        mother.

The expert went. His mission was complete.
World-masters keep him where he may be
    found,
To scorch the whole earth after man's retreat,
Burning the last generation back to the ground.

Sparrow

I pulled the sparrow's nest ravelling down with the
    ivy
That clawed my wall; less than half-made: he'll
    build
Another, I thought. But look, this little fury
With a beak attacks my window. Day and night
He hammers protest: he's cracked a pane. The life
Within a life, how it squanders itself at a wrong,
Even if the world never knew the wrong was done,
Or even, half-guilty, covered its face and turned.

So this small fledged prehistoric, tapping its flint
At a heartless glazed-in god, reminds me of
The limitless rages that we have learned to still:—
Outwardly: but they shudder within; they take on
The heart-valves and the very pulse; they rule
How we live, dictate how we suddenly die.

ROBERT GRAVES

The two poems are new ones and all I can say about them is that nobody ever wrote them before I did. They were both written in 1970 and are not yet published in volume form. I have to assume that readers are aware of the Latin meaning of genius, *which is the sense of male honour born with a man and protecting him throughout his life; and that Solomon's seal is the Arabic word for what is incorrectly called 'the Shield of David': namely a male triangle imposed on a female triangle, which is the two-dimensional sign for a double pyramid, the nether one being female and representing the Pharaoh's matrilineal right to reign. It will be recalled that Solomon, not David, married into the Pharaonic family.*

∽∾∽∾∽∾

Powers Unconfessed

Diffidently, when asked who might I be,
I agreed that, yes, I ruled a small kingdom
Though, like yourself, free to wander abroad
Hatless, barefooted and incognito.

Abruptly we embraced—a strange event,
The casual passers-by taking less notice
Than had this been a chance meeting of
    cousins—
Nor did we argue over protocol.

You, from your queendom, answerable only
To royal virtue, not to a male code,
Knew me for supernatural, like yourself,
And fell at once head over heels in love;
As I also with you—but lamentably
Never confessed what wrathful powers attest
The Roman jealousy of my male genius.

Solomon's Seal

Peace is at last confirmed for us:
A double blessing, heavily priced,
Won back as we renew our maiden hearts
In a magic known to ourselves only,
Proof against furious tides of error
And bitter ironies of the self-damned:

Perfect in love now, though not sharing
The customary pillow—and our reasons
Appear shrouded in dark Egyptian dreams
That recreate us as a single being
Wholly in love with love.

Under each pyramid lies inverted
Its twin, the sister-bride to Pharaoh,
And so Solomon's seal bears witness.

Therefore we neither plead nor threaten
As lovers do who have lost faith—
Lovers not riven together by an oath
Sworn on the very brink of birth,
Nor by the penetrative ray of need
Piercing our doubled pyramid to its bed.

All time lies knotted here in Time's caress,
And so Solomon's seal bears witness.

THOM GUNN

*I choose these two poems—'The Wound' and 'Three'—
because I still like them. The first was written about 1952:
it makes a statement, in terms of dream and mythology,
about an attempt to deal with primitive and mysterious
impulses, and about the failure of that attempt. The other
was written fifteen years later, and it is about something
perhaps related, the adult's attempt to repossess innocence,
an attempt here partially successful.*

∞∞∞∞∞

The Wound

The huge wound in my head began to heal
About the beginning of the seventh week.
Its valleys darkened, its villages became still:
For joy I did not move and dared not speak;
Not doctors would cure it, but time, its patient
　　skill.

And constantly my mind returned to Troy.
After I sailed the seas I fought in turn
On both sides, sharing even Helen's joy
Of place, and growing up—to see Troy burn—
As Neoptolemus, that stubborn boy.

I lay and rested as prescription said.
Manoeuvred with the Greeks, or sallied out

Each day with Hector. Finally my bed
Became Achilles' tent, to which the lout
Thersites came reporting numbers dead.

I was myself: subject to no man's breath:
My own commander was my enemy.
And while my belt hung up, sword in the sheath,
Thersites shambled in and breathlessly
Cackled about my friend Patroclus' death.

I called for armour, rose, and did not reel.
But, when I thought, rage at his noble pain
Flew to my head, and turning I could feel
My wound break open wide. Over again
I had to let those storm-lit valleys heal.

Three

All three are bare.
The father towels himself by two grey boulders
    Long body, then long hair,
Matted like rainy bracken, to his shoulders.

    The pull and risk
Of the Pacific's touch is yet with him:
    He kicked and felt it brisk,
Its cold live sinews tugging at each limb.

    It haunts him still:
Drying his loins, he grins to notice how,
    Struck helpless with the chill,
His cock hangs tiny and withdrawn there now.

    Near, eyes half-closed,
The mother lies back on the hot round stones,
    Her weight to theirs opposed
And pressing them as if they were earth's bones.

Hard bone, firm skin,
She holds her breasts and belly up, now dry,
Striped white where clothes have been,
To the heat that sponsors all heat, from the sky.

Only their son
Is brown all over. Rapt in endless play,
In which all games make one,
His three-year nakedness is everyday.

Swims as dogs swim.
Rushes his father, wriggles from his hold.
His body, which is him,
Sturdy and volatile, runs off the cold.

Runs up to me:
Hi there hi there, he shrills, yet will not stop,
For though continually
Accepting everything his play turns up

He still leaves it
And comes back to that pebble-warmed recess
In which the parents sit,
At watch, who had to learn their nakedness.

SEAMUS HEANEY

I find it difficult to make a decision about which poems to include, but will settle uneasily for 'The Peninsula' and 'Bogland' from Door into the Dark. *These two, I hope, by an act of attention, turn a landscape into an image and that image, in turn, has implications beyond the poem. 'Bogland' is an attempt to make the preserving, shifting marshes of Ireland a mythical landscape, a symbol of the preserving, shifting consciousness of the Irish people. History is the soft ground that holds and invites us into itself, century after century. 'The Peninsula' I like because of its fidelity to the Ards Peninsula in County Down, and also because the clarity and plainness of this landscape in the poem seems to insinuate that patience and simplicity are fundamentals.*

∽∾∽∾∽∾

Bogland

for T. P. Flanagan

We have no prairies
To slice a big sun at evening—
Everywhere the eye concedes to
Encroaching horizon,

Is wooed into the cyclops' eye
Of a tarn. Our unfenced country

Is bog that keeps crusting
Between the sights of the sun.

They've taken the skeleton
Of the Great Irish Elk
Out of the peat, set it up
An astounding crate full of air.

Butter sunk under
More than a hundred years
Was recovered salty and white.
The ground itself is kind, black butter

Melting and opening underfoot,
Missing its last definition
By millions of years.
They'll never dig coal here,

Only the waterlogged trunks
Of great firs, soft as pulp.
Our pioneers keep striking
Inwards and downwards,

Every layer they strip
Seems camped on before.
The bogholes might be Atlantic seepage.
The wet centre is bottomless.

The Peninsula

When you have nothing more to say, just drive
For a day all round the peninsula.
The sky is tall as over a runway,
The land without marks so you will not arrive

But pass through, though always skirting landfall.
At dusk, horizons drink down sea and hill,
The ploughed field swallows the whitewashed gable
And you're in the dark again. Now recall

The glazed foreshore and silhouetted log,
That rock where breakers shredded into rags,
The leggy birds stilted on their own legs,
Islands riding themselves out into the fog

And drive back home, still with nothing to say
Except that now you will uncode all landscapes
By this: things founded clean on their own shapes,
Water and ground in their extremity.

JOHN HEATH-STUBBS

I composed 'Canso' after returning from a visit to the Shrine of the Three Marys at the mouth of the River Rhône. Before retiring to bed I walked in the garden of the Communauté de Pomeyrol (a French Reformed Sisterhood in whose guest-house I was staying) near Arles. My tour in Provence that spring was my first visit to a Mediterranean country. Everywhere the colours had the vividness of a Van Gogh painting. But this very intensity seemed to enhance the underlying feeling of the presence of death, and to suggest the unreality of the visible world. I felt I had a clue to the passion of the troubadour poets, and the world-rejection of the Albigensian heretics. And I saw why in the crypt of the church of the Three Marys was the shrine of the Black Sara, goddess of the dark moon. (The Assyrian Christians still call the moon Sara.)

On that warm evening the verses seemed to come into my head quite spontaneously. They are meant to suggest the rhythm of troubadour poetry, of a medieval Provençal canso. I am afraid there is no such word as 'olivaster'. I had confused the Greek oleaster (wild olive) with the French olivâter (olive-green). But I had to let it stand for the sake of the sound.

'Plato and the Waters of the Flood', in spite of its rather elaborate form, also seemed to come into my head very spontaneously while walking in Kensington Gardens after breakfast. I had read the passage from Guthrie's book on Orphism about a week previously. Suddenly the image of Plato and the waters came to me as a symbol of the conflict between the abstract and ordering intellect and those inchoate forces within and about us from which

poetry takes its source. The intellect is compelled to reject chaos, as Plato expelled the poets from the Republic. Hence the poets take sides with those forces which oppose order, and identify with the ten-horned, seven-headed Beast from the abyss. This is a conflict which goes on continually in my own personality, and I think has been going on in our culture ever since the Greeks invented the world of abstract ideas. The poem is only one way of looking at the conflict. I have written others from an opposite point of view—notably one called 'Theseus on Naxos' composed a few months before this one.

∞∞∞∞∞

Canso

When spring airs fondle
And the nightingale
In the olivaster
   Harbours and sings,
And the moon's candle
Numinous and pale
Hangs high to foster
   Increase of things—

My heart discourses
Contrariwise:
How beauty is fallible
   In all her pride;
The season passes;
Embrowns the rose;
Nothing perdurable,
   Things faint and fade.

Thus our mortality
Fortune derides;

For love's mutations
    We learn to weep;
And no sodality
But it corrodes
Through time's collusions,
    Darkness, and sleep.

So we, being homeless
When spring rides high,
Should make obeisance
    In her cool vault
To the grave goddess
Of the moonless sky,
That her beneficence
Go not by default.

It is convenient
We take this guise
To hold her revered;
    That in all terms,
She may be lenient,
And we, likewise,
Not unprepared
    When winter comes.

Les Saintes-Maries-de-la-Mer
April 1953

Plato and the Waters of the Flood

*In one of the remoter parts of Asia Minor, near what was
once the southern boundary of the Phrygians, there is a
warm spring flanked by a Hittite monument, and known
to the Turks as Plato's Spring. The reason for the name
is that it was at this spot, according to Arab legend, that*

When on Armenian Ararat
  Or Parnassus ridge
Scrunched the overloaded keel,
  Pelican, ostrich,
Toad, rabbit, and pangolin—
  All the beasts of the field—
Scrambled out to possess once more
  Their cleansed and desolate world,
     Plato, by that fountain,
       Spoke to the swirling deep:
     'Retire, you waters of Chaos,
       Flow retrograde, and sleep;
     Above the swift revolving heavens
       Rule the intelligible,
     Chaste and undecaying ideas;
       Brackish waters, fall!'

Plato, in the academic grove,
  Among the nightingales,
Expounded to wide-eyed ephebes
  His geometric rules;
Reared a republic in the mind
  Where only noble lies
Reign; he expelled the poets
  (With courtesy, with praise).
     Loaded with useless garlands,
       Down to that fountain
     The exiled poets proceeded:
       'When will you rise again,
     Ten-horned, seven-headed seraphim,
       Out of your abyss,
     Against the beautiful Republic—
       Nor tamed by Plato's kiss?'

PHILIP HOBSBAUM

*I choose 'The Rock Pool' and 'The Ice Skaters' because I
seem to have a reputation for writing solely about violence
and disease. In fact I am deeply interested in childhood
(the subject of the first of these poems) and in human
relationships (the subject of the second, though it is also a
child-piece).*

*My friend, the Irish poet Michael Longley, told me
that the shortest book in the language would be Hobs-
baum's Verses for Children. I hope not. I often like to write
in analogy or metaphor, sideways-on to the experience.
And the metaphors I choose are, as often as not, drawn
from the period of my own childhood.*

✥✥✥✥✥

The Rock Pool

My life could have ended then, crouched over the pool,
Wedged against Huntcliff. Absorbed in its own life,
Its pimpled sea-fronds and the slimy rocks
Spangled with barnacles, the pool lay
Deceptively clear to the sky, its wraiths of weed,
Its floating upturned dead snails, the limpets
Solidly bossed to the rock—I tried to prise them
Into a free float, but cut my fingers
And winced. Deep in the clefts stiff with mussels
I pried, and under the weed that carpeted

The pool bottom recoiled from a starfish, waylaid
A crab—there he glared, squeezed little face
Tucked under his shell. And never noticed till
A wave sploshed into my pool, stirring up sludge,
Swathing crab, starfish, limpets too, in fog,
That the tide had come up, to my ears soundlessly,
Warning me off to my world, away from the sea.

The Ice Skaters

They merrily weave over the blue transparency,
Fir trees against snow-threatening sky etched
Nicely in, curvet, chassé, and slide

Merrily off—a long take, this time. I see them
Shining blonde and lustrous dark and honey-
coloured meet, escape, pirouette, and off again

Over the smooth hard sheen. Under their legs
Twirling so merrily what deep acres live
Of dark or weed or slow fish nudging past,

What bottom-sods of mud, what tangles of weed—
They slide over the surface, beckoning us on,
Gingerly we follow, test the security—fine,

They call, weaving away merrily. You
Venture to catch them up, reach out, and
Find yourself struggling in dirty water. Call,

Ice in your mouth, spluttering blindly down,
Down into the mud, entangling with weed you go.
Their laughter tinkles prettily over the ice.

DAVID HOLBROOK

The discipline involved in writing a poem often seems to me to be that of capturing the essence of a moment, with as few strokes of the brush as possible. By the 'essence' I mean those aspects of an experience that seemed at the time to gather together to form a meaning. When a poem 'labours' it often seems to be because one is trying to capture such a moment, in its complexity—but straining too much, and not capturing the touches one seeks.

I choose 'Shall These Bones Live?' and 'Day with Infant' because they seem reasonably successful in bringing together, into a pattern of meaning, aspects selected from an experience. Reading one's poems aloud to an audience helps one to see where one has done this, and where one has failed. 'Shall These Bones Live?' stands up well, I find, to being read aloud.

The actual moment was one in which, in spite of the unpromising day and the irony of the children about such expeditions, something memorable emerged. We were two agnostics peering into a box full of the burnt bones of pagans—in a setting which represented all around us the long, long struggle of man to find meaning in his life. We are part of this process, in our way, just as the German photographers are, and the old woman who collects her tips. The setting is that typically Italian one in which so many mingled things are all brought together on to the same plane, though some are mundane and others are spiritual. The little shroud tied on the cross because of Passion Week, the smell of dung, the cooking smells, the sacred paintings, the olive-oil jars, the piano and bits of harrow—all these seem to belong to the same active search for a sense of being alive, as do the pagan sculpture and the Christian art superimposed on it. Yet for us the feeling of being alive, in love, and in spring, is more important still—doomed though we are to become, ourselves, eventually, only bones in a box. One of the elements in the poem for me is the chirpy indifference of the children, who are simply content with being alive, and don't want to join us in our morbidity and awareness of man's mortal condition.

'Day with Infant' is an attempt to write about domestic life, using the same technique of bringing together fragments of the experiences of an ordinary day, beneath the surface of which are deep feelings, about death and mortality, though the actual experiences that set these feelings off are trivial. For instance, the small boy cheerfully destroys the dandelions. I have tried to kill these with poisons, but they survive. He quite brutally snaps them. The milk oozing out of them reminds one of bodily contents, and so of a whole host of primitive feelings—feelings which have to do with all the dread of annihilation touched on in the previous stanza. Yet there I have spoken of the loss of my father and mother, and other disturbing experiences, of the strange effect of a new baby's demands on one, and my wife's post-natal depression. Even on this calm, delightful day, if I reminisce, I find myself recalling dreadfulness. Yet here I am with my infant son who rushes about the garden, comic, indifferent, lovable—obviously very much alive. So I can feel that I am (at least) alive, too. In this there are profound satisfactions, and I try to conclude that my universe, despite the inevitable pain and loss involved in existing, is benign.

∾∾∾∾∾

Shall These Bones Live?

Cellole: Chiesa Romanica

So discouraging, the trouncing rain
Teeming across the burnt sienna of Tuscany.
Perhaps we can look at some churches?
So, the car winds to Cellole.
The children we leave in the car, eating hard pears in
the back.

'Call us if anything's interesting!'
You and I splat in the pools, your umbrella
Strummed like a silk drum under the hesitant chestnuts.
We shake ourselves, in the chill of the stone interior,
And you shiver in your white raincoat, pale with the
April morning.

A clink of coins in a box, and a wisp of a peasant woman
Bows off two German photographers, then dives at us,
Her face like a bright shrivelled apple, wrapped in her
black headscarf.

'*Ecco!*' The carvings, electric lit, are lucent, like butter-
sculpture;
She pidgins a thousand years of history for us:
'*Pagani!*' So it is! All around, the sun symbols.
Why does the little woman mimic a going-to-sleep?
The rings that embroider the apse are so full of life!
Ah, she awakes, to the cross, tied in its Passion Week
muff,
Crosses herself, darts through a side door; the sun comes
out.

The yard outside steams; smells of dung, cooking oil, and
garlic:
Two paintings of saints in torment, a piano, field imple-
ments:

Where the church abuts on the farm, fat oil-jars loom in
    the yard.

She briskly bends to a box hewn from alabaster—
A whole line of them stored here, carved with the same
    sun symbol—
Lifting the top, like the lid of a milk-vendor's pail.
'*Oss*'! *Oss*'!' waves a split thigh-bone at us
'*Si*!' we cry, '*Oss*'! *Pagani*!' She slaps the lid down, shoos
    a chicken.

I fumble with *lire* pieces, wondering what she expects.
Did she growl at the coins I gave her, or was it a groan
    in the door?
Good, she waves: '*Buon giorno*!' The children's breath
    steams up the car.
'Was there anything interesting?' You and I laugh and
    shout '*Oss*'!'
Behind us sardonic sighs, as, wet with spring rain, our
    mouths kiss.

Day with Infant

Calms of the sunshine: in the meadow beyond
The sloe's in frothy white blossom: the grass-smell again!
Tom trundles past on a tricycle on the new-mown grass.
He cannot pedal and sit down yet.
If he thinks of his short legs, working alternately,
He cannot remember the brake. If he thinks of either
He ceases to steer. So, giddy trajectories,
Some ending in disaster, blue jeans waving feebly.
But the white-blobbed martins have returned
And it is gentle May-time. There's no danger.

His flushed transparent doll-face
Turning to me, with round blue eyes in triumph
Under the mop of fine white dirty hair
Is a boy's determined character, even when pale and
    bruised.

Only in sleep does he become again that heavenly
    changeling
The angel-image, squeezed out from your womb that
    night
Cheesy with grease, solemn and original,
His perfect mouth-bow enigmatic as the face of God.
So, for three years, like all playing mothers and fathers,
We knelt before him, in our insane delusion,
'O unformed one, do not eat us because of our imperfec-
    tions!'
Now—I'd just like to see him try!

He follows me about today in the sunshine:
Noisy doll weighing some thirty pounds and asking
    questions,
Trampling on my first barely risen row of peas.

In my mind I try to remember the milk days:
I whirl back through dull storms, blizzards and gales:
The sky is black, and you are in dejection.
Many ghosts menace me—his embryonic psyche;
You, suffering depression in your care for him: third,
His dying grandfather, living 'on borrowed time',
From whom we tried so long to hide our grief
As all of us waited till the last pang came.
And a fourth, further yet, a long familiar ghost,
Whose death first filled this garden space with chasms.

Tom snaps the yellow dandelions that flout my poisons
And messes with their stem-milk. As I lift
His body with its belly, puppy-soft, I feel
The sun strong on us both. A charming wind

85

stirs up the dust where the fresh nettles rise.
The trees are not in leaf yet: in the calm
I feel my sweat run coolly: I am alive.

I wish I could forget. I do forget, but then,
I am guilty at forgetting. Tom must run,
Bursting away from my kisses, to be free.
And here you come, grinning, so happily:
How lovely the great calms! The indisputable joy!

TED HUGHES

'Second Glance at a Jaguar'. I choose this because it is the
sole representative among my poems of a kind of poem I
like—it is a sketch, and I wrote it standing in front of the
cage. It includes one line rejected from another poem
about a jaguar written six years before.*

'Full Moon and Little Frieda'. I choose this as one of
my favourites.*

∽∽∽∽∽∽

Second Glance at a Jaguar

Skinfull of bowls, he bowls them,
The hip going in and out of joint, dropping the spine
With the urgency of his hurry
Like a cat going along under thrown stones, under
    cover,
Glancing sideways, running
Under his spine. A terrible, stump-legged waddle
Like a thick Aztec disemboweller,
Club-swinging, trying to grind some square
Socket between his hind legs round,
Carrying his head like a brazier of spilling embers,
And the black bit of his mouth, he takes it
Between his back teeth, he has to wear his skin out,
He swipes a lap at the water-trough as he turns,

Swivelling the ball of his heel on the polished spot,
Showing his belly like a butterfly,
At every stride he has to turn a corner
In himself and correct it. His head
Is like the worn down stump of another whole jaguar,
His body is just the engine shoving it forward,
Lifting the air up and shoving on under,
The weight of his fangs hanging the mouth open,
Bottom jaw combing the ground. A gorged look,
Gangster, club-tail lumped along behind gracelessly,
He's wearing himself to heavy ovals,
Muttering some mantrah, some drum-song of murder
To keep his rage brightening, making his skin
Intolerable, spurred by the rosettes, the cain-brands,
Wearing the spots off from the inside,
Rounding some revenge. Going like a prayer-wheel,
The head dragging forward, the body keeping up,
The hind legs lagging. He coils, he flourishes
The blackjack tail as if looking for a target,
Hurrying through the underworld, soundless.

Full Moon and Little Frieda

A cool small evening shrunk to a dog bark and
        the clank of a bucket—

And you listening.
A spider's web, tense for the dew's touch.
A pail lifted, still and brimming—mirror
To tempt a first star to a tremor.

Cows are going home in the lane there, looping the
        hedges with their warm wreaths of breath—
A dark river of blood, many boulders,
Balancing unspilled milk.

'Moon!' you cry suddenly, 'Moon! Moon!'

The moon has stepped back like an artist gazing
    amazed at a work
That points at him amazed.

ELIZABETH JENNINGS

The two poems I choose are 'For a Child Born Dead' and 'Fountain', both from my Collected Poems. *I choose the first of these because it was written in a quite different way from my usual habit. My sister lost a baby and, four days later, I wrote this poem straight, with scarcely any alterations at all. This last is not unusual, but it is unusual for me to write so close to an event.*

'Fountain' was written straight out on Maundy Thursday in Rome one year during the late 1950s. It quite literally flowed out but, though it has no set form, it has, I believe, an inner intensity, in other words it is not vers libre. It is not about any particular fountain in Rome: it is really about power—*something which had been vexing me and which I had been trying to get into my poetry for a year or two. In 'Fountain' I feel I succeeded in doing this.*

∞∞∞∞

For a Child Born Dead

What ceremony can we fit
You into now? If you had come
Out of a warm and noisy room
To this, there'd be an opposite
For us to know you by. We could
Imagine you in lively mood

And then look at the other side,
The mood drawn out of you, the breath
Defeated by the power of death.
But we have never seen you stride
Ambitiously the world we know.
You could not come and yet you go.

But there is nothing now to mar
Your clear refusal of our world.
Not in our memories can we mould
You or distort your character.
Then all our consolation is
That grief can be as pure as this.

Fountain

Let it disturb no more at first
Than the hint of a pool predicted far in a forest,
Or a sea so far away that you have to open
Your window to hear it.
Think of it then as elemental, as being
Necessity,
Not for a cup to be taken to it and not
For lips to linger or eye to receive itself
Back in reflection, simply
As water the patient moon persuades and stirs.

And then step closer,
Imagine rivers you might indeed embark on,
Waterfalls where you could
Silence an afternoon by staring but never
See the same tumult twice.
Yes come out of the narrow street and enter
The full piazza. Come where the noise compels.
Statues are bowing down to the breaking air.

Observe it there——the fountain, too fast for shadows,
Too wild for the lights which illuminate it to hold,
Even a moment, an ounce of water back;
Stare at such prodigality and consider
It is the elegance here, it is the taming,
The keeping fast in a thousand flowering sprays,
That builds this energy up but lets the watchers
See in that stress an image of utter calm,
A stillness there. It is how we must have felt
Once at the edge of some perpetual stream,
Fearful of touching, bringing no thirst at all,
Panicked by no perception of ourselves
But drawing the water down to the deepest
        wonder.

JAMES KIRKUP

'*The Core of the Matter*' *is my favourite new poem because it continues, after 25 years, my preoccupation with the theme of heart surgery which first appears in '*A Correct Compassion*'. However, there is more to my choice than this. My deep concern about the problems of racial discrimination, which have become ever more acute in England as well as in the United States, caused me to add a new dimension to the theme. The heart of a black woman in a white man's body—and a white South African policeman at that!—seemed to me a subject on which I could express myself eloquently, poetically and with illuminating irony. As I was writing the poem (at Amherst, Mass., in the autumn of 1968) many lines about the heart from other English poets sprang naturally into my mind—Shakespeare, Yeats, Sir Philip Sidney. I incorporated these lines into my own text, to act as a kind of commentary on my views from other poets. The dictionary was also pressed into service, as was the newspaper cutting itself that suggested the poem. I was therefore able to create the kind of poem I have often written, and of which I am very fond—something on a contemporary theme, treated with vision and feeling, and incorporating actual speech or prose or newspaper cuttings, and seizing upon one significant word to use throughout the poem as a refrain and a pattern. This word is 'sources'. It is a word rich in all kinds of meanings, which I hope are well displayed in this poem. I should add that the title is taken from the first line of '*A Correct Compassion*'.*

'*Lost Dog*' *is a poem I enjoyed writing, yet it was a painful experience. I am friends with the animals, and I* have written several poems about them. Secondly, I am concerned about the fate of helpless animals in our pitiless modern cities. There have recently been many outcries about the brutal and inhuman treatment given to dogs in Japan, especially in hospitals, where they are made the subjects of cruel experiments in vivisection. Once when I was lying ill in a Japanese hospital, my days and nights were made hideous by the howlings of dogs in pain because of these experiments.

Of course, in the East the general attitude towards animals is one of indifference. In Japan, dogs in the city are left chained up all day and night, with no companionship and little food, They are there just to bark, and bark they do, in a truly neurotic fashion, at every passer-by and at every other barking dog in the neighbourhood. They are kept chained up because in a huge city like Tokyo there are no suitable places to exercise them, and dog-stealers are common: they use the skins to make handbags and so on. Also, if a dog escapes from his home, or gets lost, he will be picked up by the dog-disposal squad and exterminated most inhumanely. The 'dog pounds' of Tokyo are a disgrace to a supposedly civilized nation. So whenever I see a lost dog trotting through the busy streets of Tokyo or Osaka, my heart is wrung with pity for its fate, for its growing weariness and bewilderment in a world of heartless men. I feel that, like myself, lost dogs are aliens in a strange and uncaring land, a land which the Japanese themselves now call a 'land of economic animals'. My poem therefore expresses my feelings about homeless dogs, and about homeless humans like myself who are helpless foreigners in a land grown harsh and pitiless with modernization and commercialism. But it could, of course, be almost any country today.

∞∞∞∞∞

The Core of the Matter

'A Pregnant Black was Heart Donor. Recipient
in Capetown A White Ex-policeman.'
                    (*New York Times* headline)

The sources said
Black mother with child
Delivered of her heart.

Informed hospital sources said
She had died earlier in the day.
A haemorrhage of the brain.

How did the heart survive?
What cupped its blood?
The sources do not say.

Telltale heart translated
Into the ribcage of a white
Ex-policeman, age fifty-two.

She lost her heart
But not to him to whom
She lost her heart.

We know his name, his family,
His address. Not hers.
'Sources said they did not know
Whether her family had been traced.'

All we know now is
She was black,
About thirty-two years old,
Thirty-two weeks gone.

The sources also said
They did not know
What happened to the unborn child.

A child ripped untimely
From his mother's heart.

Sources said the donor's
'Advanced state of pregnancy
Made her a suitable
Type of donor because blood
Circulation is best in pregnancy.'

Blood from a pregnant woman
Is the best juice available,
Black or white.
Black will do as well as white.
In the dark of death
All hearts are alike,
All blood is red.

All hearts are red.
The hearts of pregnant women
Are full to overflowing.

In the right place, her heart
'Started beating spontaneously
and normally,' so the sources said.

Proud to be white,
No longer anonymous?
Not mother-passioned now,
But fathered-forth?

'Hearts are not had as a gift . . .'
But hers was.
Unsolicited.

To segregate, the sources say, is 'to
Separate from the general body.'
Certainly she
Was segregated.
So was her heart.

Miscegenation of the heart
Is just exchange,
'One for the other giv'n. . . .'

But segregation
Here was integration.
'There never was a better bargain driv'n.'

—Can we take heart from this,
Learn a lesson it never tried to teach,
That black is white
And white is black

And one day
The twain shall meet?

What do the sources say?

Lost Dog

Endlessly trotting,
Stopping a second,
Not to sniff, but
To look—down a lane,
Into faces that ignore you,
Trotting on again
With that exhausted
Inexhaustibility.
You are lost, and know it.

Dogs with homes and owners
Stand and watch you
Trotting in mad traffic.
They do not speak to you.
They do not help you.
In Japan, anyone who

Does not belong is suspect.
You are an outcast.
You are lost, and know it.

Panting, pink tongue hanging
Loose from jaws parted
In a frightened smile,
Sharp ears cocked for
The voice of a man who once
Called you by name,
Tail endlessly wagging
When children stop you.
You are lost, and they know it.

But children are no good.
You know it. They
Are not masters.
They pet your impatience
With clumsy gaiety.
Grateful for the least touch
Of humanity, of warmth,
You have no spirit
To bite their cruel fingers.

A tramp in the park
Attaches himself to you,
But you feel somehow
It's no good, you are off
Endlessly trotting, up steps,
Down lanes, across highways,
Through the grounds of shrines;
Trying to look normal, you
Conceal desperation everyone sees.

Everyone sees you are lost,
And turns away from you.
Where is your famed
Japanese sense of direction?

Can't you smell your way
Home, like a cat? No,
You're not that clever.
Tokyo: demented maze of
Lights and indifference.

Night fell long ago, but still
You trot, endlessly trot. In Tokyo,
The world's biggest, but
Not greatest city, there are
So many streets, so few
Homes for the lost, the sad,
The desperate, the abandoned.
In your situation, a man
Would commit suicide.

A face, a voice, a stroking hand
That you will never know again—
These are the memories you run to.
Scraps in the gutters disgust you:
You drink the water scattered
In front of shops to lay the dust.
Why have you no collar,
No name, no address?
Yes, you have a name. Taro.

But you can't tell it to anyone.
Besides, nearly every dog
Is called Taro in Japan.
It is a voice, not a name
You answer to. An accent.
When I call 'Taro!' you
Stop a second, wild with hope.
But the voice isn't right.
Who wants a foreigner, anyway?

What was your master's name?
Your eyes are filled with

Dumb information, the long
History of a dog's life.
Kicks, blows, fights, bruises,
Cuts, whippings, houndings by
Cats, trucks, children, cars.
Patient waitings for masters,
Scraps of dirty rice.

Now your movie
Flickers its last reel.
The fire-engines
Howl, but not for you;
Ambulances scream,
But not for you; mobile
Blood-transfusion units wail,
But not for you.
You are still lost, and know it.

The policeman halts traffic,
But not for you; signals change,
Doors open, but not for you;
Cherry blooms, but not for you;
Children wave bye-bye
But not for you.
Night falls. Night falls.
But not for you.
You are still lost, and know it.

Endlessly trotting,
You pant through the city
Of empty neon. No one
In the streets. You run
Down the middle of roads,
Your feathery tail
Waving wildly in headlamps
Of prowling taxis.
You are lost forever, and you know it.

Endlessly trotting into
The dawn of a new day.
But dawn is only
Chill neon, not the sun.
You trot endlessly on, knowing
This is your last day, knowing
This is your last light, knowing
This is your last breath, knowing
They know you are lost, they know you
　　are lost.

PHILIP LARKIN

I looked through my three books of poems, and after some time came to the conclusion that I was subconsciously looking for poems which did not seem to me to have received their due meed of praise. Of course, there were quite a lot of them, and selection was difficult, but in the end I picked 'MCMXIV' and 'Send No Money', both *from* The Whitsun Weddings.

Looking at them, I see that they have a certain superficial resemblance: they are both, for instance, in more or less the same metre. On the other hand, they might be taken as representative examples of the two kinds of poem I sometimes think I write: the beautiful and the true. I have always believed that beauty is beauty, truth truth, that is not all ye know on earth nor all ye need to know, and I think a poem usually starts off either from the feeling How beautiful that is or from the feeling How true that is. One of the jobs of the poem is to make the beautiful seem true and the true beautiful, but in fact the disguise can usually be penetrated.

∽∽∽∽∽

MCMXIV

Those long uneven lines
Standing as patiently
As if they were stretched outside
The Oval or Villa Park,

The crowns of hats, the sun
On moustached archaic faces
Grinning as if it were all
An August Bank Holiday lark;

And the shut shops, the bleached
Established names on the sunblinds,
The farthings and sovereigns,
And dark-clothed children at play
Called after kings and queens,
The tin advertisements
For cocoa and twist, and the pubs
Wide open all day;

And the countryside not caring:
The place-names all hazed over
With flowering grasses, and fields
Shadowing Domesday lines
Under wheat's restless silence;
The differently-dressed servants
With tiny rooms in huge houses,
The dust behind limousines;

Never such innocence,
Never before or since,
As changed itself to past
Without a word—the men
Leaving the gardens tidy,
The thousands of marriages
Lasting a little while longer:
Never such innocence again.

Send No Money

Standing under the fobbed
Independent belly of Time
Tell me the truth, I said,
Teach me the way things go.
All the other lads there
Were itching to have a bash,
But I thought wanting unfair:
It and finding out clash.

So he patted my head, booming *Boy*,
There's no green in your eye:
Sit here, and watch the hail
Of occurrence clobber life out
To a shape no one sees—
Dare you look at that straight?
Oh thank you, I said, *Oh yes please*,
And sat down to wait.

Half life is over now,
And I meet full face on dark mornings
The bestial visor, bent in
By the blows of what happened to happen.
What does it prove? Sod all.
In this way I spent youth,
Tracing the trite untransferable
Truss-advertisement, truth.

LAURIE LEE

I have chosen these two poems because they are perhaps less known than others of mine, and also because they have always had a particular effect on me: the first, 'Black Edge', because it was a direct cry made at the edge of breakdown, and one which, because I was able to make it, may have saved me at the time; the second, 'Bird', because it seems to have been one of those mysteries familiar to most writers of poetry—something that wrote itself instantly, as though dictated from some unknown source, and which has always remained for me haunting and never fully understood.

∽∽∽∽∽

Black Edge

I lie no more in a healthy sheet,
a wind of chill eyes makes a marsh of my cheeks,
diseased is my sleep with demented sound
and I am infected by the stars.

For see how the sun rubs ulcers in the sky
how black as bats the field flowers droop and fall;
the earth, the sweet earth,
is foul and full of graves.

O save me, for I am sick;
lay on my eyelids your finger's miracle,
bewitch me that I may live.

105

Wash me in happy air,
restore me with the odours of rivers;
then feed, O feed
my sight with your normal love.

Bird

O bird that was my vision,
my love, my dream that flew
over the famine-folded rocks,
the sky's reflected snow.

O bird that found and fashioned me,
that brought me from the land
safe in her singing cage of bone,
the webbed wings of her hand.

She took me to the topmost air,
curled in the atom of her eye,
and there I saw an island rise
out of the empty sea.

And falling there she set me down
naked on soil that knew no plough,
and loveless, speechless, I beheld
the world's beginning grow.

And there I slew her for my bread
and in her feathers dressed;
and there I raised a paradise
from the seed in her dead breast.

C. DAY LEWIS

May I suggest as my two poems the last sonnet of 'O Dreams, O Destinations' (Collected Poems) and 'On Not Saying Everything' (The Room). The sonnet because, though I wrote it thirty years ago, it still stands up and says something I feel to be truthful about the human condition: 'On Not Saying Everything' because I believe so strongly in the doctrine of limitations it speaks for— that everything, a tree, a poem, a human relationship, lives and thrives by the limits imposed on it.

∽∽∽∽∽∽

From *O Dreams, O Destinations*

9

To travel like a bird, lightly to view
Deserts where stone gods founder in the sand,
Ocean embraced in a white sleep with land;
To escape time, always to start anew.
To settle like a bird, make one devoted
Gesture of permanence upon the spray
Of shaken stars and autumns; in a bay
Beyond the crestfallen surges to have floated.
Each is our wish. Alas, the bird flies blind,
Hooded by a dark sense of destination:
Her weight on the glass calm leaves no impression,
Her home is soon a basketful of wind.
Travellers, we're fabric of the road we go;
We settle, but like feathers on time's flow.

On Not Saying Everything

This tree outside my window here,
Naked, umbrageous, fresh or sere,
Has neither chance nor will to be
Anything but a linden tree,
Even if its branches grew to span
The continent; for nature's plan
Insists that infinite extension
Shall create no new dimension.
From the first snuggling of the seed
In earth, a branchy form's decreed.

Unwritten poems loom as if
They'd cover the whole of earthly life.
But each one, growing, learns to trim its
Impulse and meaning to the limits
Roughed out by me, then modified
In its own truth's expanding light.
A poem, settling to its form,
Finds there's no jailer, but a norm
Of conduct, and a fitting sphere
Which stops it wandering everywhere.

As for you, my love, it's harder,
Though neither prisoner nor warder,
Not to desire you both: for love
Illudes us we can lightly move
Into a new dimension, where
The bounds of being disappear
And we make one impassioned cell.
So wanting to be all in all
Each for each, a man and woman
Defy the limits of what's human.

Your glancing eye, your animal tongue,
Your hands that flew to mine and clung

Like birds on bough, with innocence
Masking those young experiments
Of flesh, persuaded me that nature
Formed us each other's god and creature.
Play out then, as it should be played,
The sweet illusion that has made
An eldorado of your hair
And our love an everywhere.

But when we cease to play explorers
And become settlers, clear before us
Lies the next need—to re-define
The boundary between yours and mine;
Else, one stays prisoner, one goes free.
Each to his own identity
Grown back, shall prove our love's expression
Purer for this limitation.
Love's essence, like a poem's, shall spring
From the not saying everything.

EDWARD LUCIE-SMITH

The reasons for my choice are, I suppose, mildly capricious, as more and more I find that I don't have special favourites among my own poems. Each is an experience, more or less satisfactorily embodied for the reader. New poems are more interesting to me than old ones, but only because they are new, and therefore 'nearer'.

'The Hermit to His Cat'. This comes from a sequence of poems, originally meant to be set to music, about a hermit in the early middle ages, who lives as a solitary on a rocky island, perhaps off the Atlantic coast of Ireland. The hermit himself speaks in each of the poems, which are all in different forms, and the cycle takes him through a single day's existence, from waking with the dawn to lying awake again at midnight. The poem touches—lightly, I hope—on theological arguments about the nature of grace and whether or not an animal can be said to have a soul. The 'natural' cruelty of animals makes us see the world's evil (indeed, it embodies some part of the world's evil, which is the consequence of the Fall). On the other hand, animals themselves are sinless, unlike man. Hence the complicated pun on 'grace' at the end of the poem.

'The Son'. The embodiment of a story told to me by a close friend, and an attempt to exorcize it from my own mind. It contrasts with 'The Hermit to His Cat' by being straight reporting, not an embodiment through a fiction.

∞∞∞∞∞

The Hermit to His Cat

Old Nick! Mephisto!
Dear Companion!
You, with your devil's
Look and voice. Poor puss!
Poor puss! How many
Years alone with me?
You speak, and I. We
Understand the tone,
The glance, but do not
Know what has been said.

I catch you fish. You
Warm my bed. I see
Hell in those yellow
Eyes; and when you trace
Your patterns round a
Wounded gull it's how
The devil comes to kill.
All steel! All velvet!
You prove that Satan
Too is part of grace.

The Son

Lying awake, in the room
Over their room, the voices
Drifting up through the floor-boards—
A grinding, night-long quarrel
Between the two who made you.
How can you bear to listen?

A shared bed, a shared hatred
To warm it in the small hours.

Four living children, one dead.
Five proofs of something, one you
Who lie there above them. Grey
Coals hiss as the fire burns low.

GEORGE MacBETH

The two poems I have chosen—'Scissor-Man' and 'When I Am Dead'—were written fast and unexpectedly. They have an odd kitchen violence which puzzles and intrigues me. Neither has been anthologized before.

Scissor-Man

I am dangerous
        in a crisis
with sharp legs and a screw

        in my genitals. I slice
bacon-rind for a living. At nights I
        lie dried

under the draining-board, dreaming
        of Nutcrackers
and the Carrot-grater. If I should

        catch him rubbing
those tin nipples of hers
        in the bread-bin

(God rust his pivot!) so much for
        secrecy. I'd have his
washer off. And

        then what? It scarcely pays
to be 'Made in Hamburg'. Even
        our little salt-spoon

can sound snooty
        with an E.P.N.S. under
his arm-pit. Even the pie-server

        who needs re-dipping. In sixteen
stainless years dividing
        chippolata links I

am still denied
        a place in the sink unit. And
you can imagine

        what pairing-off is possible
with a wriggle of cork-screws
        in an open knife-box. So I

keep my legs
        crossed. I never cut up
rough. I lie with care

        in a world where a squint leg
could be fatal. I sleep like a weapon
        with a yen for a pierced ear.

When I Am Dead

I desire that my body be
properly clothed. In such things
as I may like at the time.

And in the pockets may there be
placed such things as I use at the time
as, pen, camera, wallet, file.

And I desire to be laid on my side
face down: since I have bad dreams
if I lie on my back.

No one shall see my face when I die.

And beside me shall lie
my stone pig
with holes in his eyes.

And the coffin shall be as big as a crate.
No thin box
for the bones only.

Let there be room for a rat to come in.

And see that my cat, if I have one then,
shall have my liver.
He will like that.

And lay in food for
a week and a day:
chocolate, meat, beans, cheese.

And let all lie in
the wind and the rain.
And on the eighth day burn.

And the ash
scatter as the wind decides.
And the stone and metal be dug in the ground.

This is my will.

ROGER McGOUGH

My reasons for the choice of these two poems are perhaps irrational, in that, at the time of going to press, neither had been published before, and my favourite poems are always those nearest at hand and crying out for air.

'George and the Dragonfly' is based part on truth, part on fantasy. There was a boy I knew at school who was gifted like the one in the poem (although his targets were not confined to dragonflies, and I doubt if he grew to acquire a taste for sherry and suntanned friends). Everybody is good at something, and I suppose this poem is about children being good at things which society later deems unimportant. And I think it's a pity.

I chose the second poem mainly because it was thin. 'George and the Dragonfly' is a fat poem and when I was writing it I could hear birds singing. When I wrote 'Crusader' the birds had stopped.

∞∞∞∞∞

George and the Dragonfly

Georgie Jennings was spit almighty.
When the golly was good
he could down a dragonfly at 30 feet
and drown a 100 midges with the fallout.
At the drop of a cap
he would outspit lads
years older and twice his size.
Freckled and rather frail

116

he assumed the quiet dignity
beloved of schoolboy heroes.

But though a legend in his own playtime
Georgie Jennings failed miserably in the
    classroom
and left school at 15 to work for his father.
And talents such as spitting
are considered unbefitting
for upandcoming porkbutchers.

I haven't seen him since,
but like to imagine some summer soiree
when, after a day moistening mince,
George and his wife entertain tanned friends.
And after dinner, sherrytongued talk
drifts back to schooldays
the faces halfrecalled, the adventures
overexaggerated. And the next thing
that shy sharpshooter of days gone by
is led, vainly protesting, on to the lawn,
where, in the hush of a golden August evening
a reputation, 20 years tall, is put to the test.
So he takes extra care as yesterheroes must,
fires, and a dragonfly, incapsulated, bites the
    dust.
Then amidst bravos and tinkled applause,
blushing, Georgie leads them back indoors.

Crusader

in bed
like a dead
crusader

arms folded a
cross my chest
i lie

eyes closed
listening
to the bodys glib mechanics

* * *

on the street
outside
men of violence

quarrel
their drunken voices
dark weals

on the
glistening
back of the night

NORMAN NICHOLSON

I choose 'From a Boat at Coniston' because I think it expresses a difficulty which faces all poets when they try to write about the natural world—a doubt as to whether they can ever see it objectively or just see themselves reflected in it.

'Have You Been to London?' is a more recent poem. It is a memory of the time when I used to go to my grandmother's, once a week, to read to her, though I did not realize until years after she was dead that she herself had never learned to read. By the 'little literate boys' at the end who hadn't learned to close doors behind them I'm thinking of the scientists and technologists, who can send a man to the moon but have not yet learned how to make men live in courtesy and communion together, how to close the doors behind them in places like Vietnam.

∞∞∞∞∞

From a Boat at Coniston

I look into the lake (the lacquered water
Black with the sunset), watching my own face.
Tiny red-ribbed fishes swim
In and out of the nostrils, long-tongued weeds
Lick at the light that oozes down from the
    surface,
And bubbles rise from the eyes like aerated

Tears shed there in the element of mirrors.
My sight lengthens its focus; sees the sky
Laid level upon the glass, the loud
World of the wind and the map-making clouds
    and history
Squinting over the rim of the fell. The wind
Lets on the water, paddling like a duck,
And face and cloud are grimaced out
In inch-deep wrinkles of the moving waves.
A blackbird clatters; alder leaves
Make mooring buoys for the water beetles.
I wait for the wind to drop, against hope
Hoping, and against the weather, yet to see
The water empty, the water full of itself,
Free of the sky and the cloud and free of me.

Have You Been to London?

'Have you been to London?'
My grandmother asked me.
          'No.'—
China dogs on the mantelshelf,
Paper blinds at the window,
Three generations simmering on the
    bright black lead,
And a kettle filled to the neb,
Spilled over long ago.

I blew into the room, threw
My scholarship cap on the rack;
Wafted visitors up the flue
With the draught of my coming in—
Ready for Saturday's mint imperials,
Ready to read
The serial in 'Titbits', the evangelical

Tale in the parish magazine,
Under the green
Glare of the gas,
Under the stare of my grandmother's
   Queen.

My grandmother burnished her sleek
   steel hair—
Not a tooth in her jaw
Nor alphabet in her head,
Her spectacles lost before I was born,
Her lame leg stiff in the sofa corner,
Her crutch at the steady:
'They shut doors after them
In London,' she said.

I crossed the hearth and thumped
   the door *to*;
Then turned to Saturday's stint,
My virtuosity of print
And grandmother's wonder:
Reading of throttler and curate,
Blood, hallelujahs and thunder,
While the generations boiled down
   to one
And the kettle burnt dry
In a soon grandmotherless room;

Reading for forty years,
Till the print swirled out like a
   down-catch of soot
And the wind howled round
A world left cold and draughty,
Un-latched, un-done,
By all the little literate boys
Who hadn't been to London.

BRIAN PATTEN

I don't really know why I write poems, there are no rules about it, I simply write them and am glad to have written them. Sometimes they are happy poems, sometimes they are a bit sad and a bit too serious, but still they are poems. They are a way of recording what you have seen and felt; they are saying 'I am glad to be alive, no matter what that life is like.'

The first poem 'Interruption at the Opera House' is a story poem, and for me it says simply that the world and all in it should be shared, that no one small section of people should have a monopoly over life. Other people reading the poem might think it means something similar but different. In such poems more than one meaning can be found. It would perhaps be a bad poem if it had only one meaning.

Maybe the same can be said for the second poem, 'Prose Poem towards a Definition of Itself'. It is what I think poetry is about. Since the poem was written I've not changed my mind about it, only now think poetry is about even more things. Things I did not know about when the poem was written are now known, and so the poem could well go on. I choose it mainly because of its strange images. The images can mean different things to different people, and this is how it should be. If you want, it's like a landscape, and though everyone can see the landscape at the same time, the things they see in it might well be different. The poem is now seven or eight times as long as the version printed here and will continue to grow and change as I grow and change. And I hope it will continue to improve. . . .

ᴏᴏᴏᴏᴏᴏ

Interruption at the Opera House

At the very beginning of an important symphony,
while the rich and famous were settling into their quietly
    expensive boxes,
a man came crashing through the crowds,
carrying in his hand a cage in which
the rightful owner of the music sat,
yellow and tiny and very poor;
and taking onto the rostrum this rather timid bird
he turned up the microphones, and it sang.

'A very original beginning to the evening,' said the
    crowds,
quietly glancing at their programmes to find
the significance of the intrusion.

Meanwhile at the box office, the organisers of the evening
were arranging for small and uniformed attendants
to evict, even forcefully, the intruders.
But as the attendants, poor and gathered from the nearby
    slums at little expense,
went rushing down the aisles to do their job
they heard above the coughing and irritable rattling of
    jewels,
a sound that filled their heads with light,
and from somewhere inside them there bubbled up a
    stream,
and there came a breeze on which their youth was carried.
How sweetly the bird sang!

And though soon the fur-wrapped crowds
were leaving their boxes and in confusion were winding
    their way home
still the attendants sat in the aisles,
and some, so delighted at what they heard, rushed out to
    call
their families and friends.

And their children came,
sleepy for it was late in the evening,
very late in the evening,
and they hardly knew if they had done with dreaming
or had begun again.
In all the tenement blocks
the lights were clicking on,
and the rightful owner of the music,
tiny and no longer timid, sang
for the rightful owners of the song.

Prose Poem towards a Definition
of Itself

When in public poetry should take off its clothes and
wave to the nearest person in sight; It should be seen in
the company of thieves and lovers rather than that of
journalists and publishers. On sighting mathematicians
it should unhook the algebra from their minds and
replace it with poetry; on sighting poets it should un-
hook poetry from the minds and replace it with algebra:
it should touch those people who despise being touched,
it should fall in love with children and woo them with
fairytales; it should wait on the landing for two years for
its mates to come home then go outside and find them all
dead.

When the electricity fails it should wear dark glasses and
pretend to be blind. It should guide those who are safe
into the middle of busy roads and leave them there. It
should scatter woodworm into the bedrooms of all peg-
legged men, not being afraid to hurt the innocent; It
should shout EVIL! EVIL! EVIL! from the roofs of
stock exchanges. It should not pretend to be a clerk or
librarian. It is the eventual sameness of contradictions.

It should never weep unless it is alone, and then only after it has covered the mirrors and sealed up the cracks. Poetry is the astronaut stepping for the first time into liquid space; it is the brilliant fish chattering in the deep pool; the bomb exploding for no particular reason over the deserted villages; the unicorn dying on the edge of the new industrial estates; the albatross laughing as at last it enters the wedding feast.

Poetry should seek out pale and lyrical couples and wander with them into stables, neglected bedrooms, engineless cars, unsafe forests, for A Final Good Time. It should enter burning factories too late to save anybody. It should pay no attention to its name.

Poetry should be seen lying by the side of road accidents, hissing from unlit gas-rings. It should scrawl the nymph's secret on her teacher's blackboard, offer her a worm saying: Inside this is a tiny apple. At dawn it should leave the bedroom and catch the first bus home to its wife. At dusk it should chat up a girl nobody wants. It should be seen standing on the ledge of a skyscraper, on a bridge with a brick tied around its heart. Poetry is the monster hiding in a child's dark room. It is the scar on a beautiful person's face. It is the last blade of grass being picked from the city park.

RUTH PITTER

I shall be glad to see 'The Swifts' in print at last. It was written on purpose to be sung, and I venture to hope some one will try to set it. It should at least be spoken aloud, and with great energy.

'Planting Mistletoe' was printed in 'Punch' long ago. It has never been collected, but I always liked it for the rich rhyme-scheme (with internals), and for the Christian analogy (the death of the tree, and, in contrast, the strange magical plant growing out of it, to provide golden foliage and pearl-like berries in tragic mid-winter).

∽∽∽∽∽

The Swifts

Flying low over the warm roof of an old barn,
Down in a flash to the water, up and away with a cry,
And a wild swoop and a swift turn
And a fever of life under a thundery sky,
So they go over, so they go by.

And high and high and high in the diamond light,
They soar and they shriek in the sunlight when
　　　heaven is bare,
With the pride of life in their strong flight
And a rapture of love to lift them, to hurtle them
　　　there,
High and high in the diamond air.

126

And away with the summer, away like the spirit of
    glee,
Flashing and calling, and strong on the wing, and
    wild in their play,
With a high cry to the high sea,
And a heart for the south, a heart for the diamond
    day,
So they go over, so go away.

Planting Mistletoe

Let the old tree be the gold tree,
Hand up the silver seed;
Let the hoary tree be the glory tree,
To shine out at need,
At mirth-time, at dearth-time,
Gold bough and milky bead.

For the fruit's going and the root's
    going,
Soon it will bloom no more.
The growth's arrested, the yaffle's*
    nested
Deep in its hollow core;
Over the grasses thinly passes
The shade so dark before.

Take a few sprigs of the new twigs,
If any such you find:
Don't lose them, but use them,
Keeping a good kind
To be rooting and fruiting
When this is old and blind.

* yaffle = Green Woodpecker

So the tragic tree is the magic tree,
Running the whole range
Of growing and blowing
And suffering change;
Then buying, by dying,
The wonderful and strange.

WILLIAM PLOMER

I have chosen 'Good-bye to the Island' because it is about a moment that occurs in many young lives, the turning-point when pleasure and idleness give way to a sense of purpose and responsibility.

It has been a great happiness for me to work with Benjamin Britten on four operatic librettos, so the destruction of the Maltings by fire, and its rebuilding, have had a special significance for me. This I have tried to convey in 'A Note from a Cello'.

∽∽∽∽∽

Good-bye to the Island

Good-bye to the island
And the view across the straits:
Work that gained us pleasure
Will now be done by others.

Good-bye to the pleasure
And the island girls
Who taught us as they fancied
And found us willing learners.

Good-bye to the fancies
Of two wandering boys,
The picnics on the mountain
Where the grass was gilt and
        brittle.

129

Good-bye to the ruins,
The tramway to the port,
The dusty moonlit suburbs,
The private rooms we rented.

A life of wine and marble
And voices in the mist
Will trouble us no longer,
The gulls are all returning.

The past was like a sculptor
Determining our will,
We grapple with the future
And shape our new intentions,

So now to the last harbour
And our easygoing ways,
To white grapes in a basket
And the island nights, good-bye.

A Note from a Cello

(The Maltings restored: 1970)

A blameless calm night, the people have gone.
Dark thickets of reeds feel a breath of disquiet:
Moorhens awake; fear saves the vole
About to be hooked by the soft-flying owl;
In the marshes of Snape a sluice and a pool
Make suddenly shapes of flame-coloured light.

Crackle of fire! An undeclared war,
Motiveless, strikes at those who contrived
That resonant shell, at ears that have heard
Rejoicings derived, in nights darker by far,
From far greater fires, wells deeper, deep dreams,
Granite, violets, blood, the pureness of dew.

The shell is restored. The orchestra settles.
A baton is raised. Renew what is old!
Make known what is new! From a cello the bow
Draws its hauntingest tone, confiding, profound:
And immured in the bone the marrow responds
To the endless, exploring inventions of sound.

PETER PORTER

It's very difficult to choose two poems to represent one's style and at the same time pick works one likes. I've avoided the things of mine which usually get into anthologies. I often use complex stanzas and rhyme schemes but these two poems are in free verse. 'The Great Poet Comes Here in Winter' is a sort of dramatic monologue or soliloquy. It's based on, though not entirely, the life of the Austrian poet Rilke. You're to think of him as having bummed (borrowed is too polite a word) a castle from one of his friends in the nobility and he is looking out over the wintry Adriatic. The poem is, in its curious way, a celebration of life. It acknowledges that life is miserable and ends in death but it finds some kind of heroic consolation in the very act of living. 'The Sadness of the Creatures' is probably gloomier. It's about human dependence, predatoriness and the fact that most of us are meat-eaters. It's also about marriage and the desolate spots in human relationships. Attila was the great Asiatic conqueror and leader of the Huns who almost destroyed Europe in the years after the fall of Rome. He has become a by-word for rapacity. El Dorado or the Golden Man was the name given to the mythical land of plenty in South America. The Massacre of the Innocents was ordered by Herod to destroy the Christ-Child. The point here is that the sufferers are not the instigators. Both poems will exhibit a tighter and less prosy rhythm if they are read aloud. These poems may seem a little esoteric but I have tried to explain them in this note. I feel, perhaps over-sensitively, that I am often misrepresented in anthologies.

∞∞∞∞

132

The Great Poet Comes
Here in Winter

Frau Antonia is a cabbage:
If I were a grub I'd eat a hole in her.
Here they deliver the milk up a private path
Slippery as spit—her goddess' hands
Turn it to milk puddings. Blow, little wind,
Steer in off this cardboard sea,
You are acclimatised like these vines
Warring on an inch of topsoil,
You are agent of the Golden Republic,
So still blow for me—our flowers look one way,
If I were a good poet I would walk on the sea.

The sea is actually made of eyes.
Whether of drowned fishermen or of peasants
Accustomed to the hard bargains of the saints
I cannot say. Whether there will be
Any mail from Paris or even broccoli
For dinner is in doubt. My hat blew off the planet,
I knelt by the infinite sand of the stars
And prayed for all men. Being German, I have a lot
      of soul.
Nevertheless, why am I crying in this garden?
I refuse to die till fashion comes back to spats.

From this turret the Adriatic
Burns down the galley lanes to starved Ragusa,
The world is coming unstitched at the seams.
All yesterday the weather was a taste
In my mouth, I saw the notes of Beethoven
Lying on the ground, from the horn
Of a gramophone I heard Crivelli's cucumbers
Crying out for paint. In the eyes of a stray bitch
Ribbed with hunger, heavy with young,
I saw the peneplain of all imagined

Misery, horizontal and wider than the world.
I gave her my unwrapped sugar. We said Mass
Together, she licking my fingers and me
Knowing how she would die, not glad to have lived.
She took her need away, I thought her selfish
But stronger than God and more beautiful company.

The Sadness of the Creatures

We live in a third floor flat
among gentle predators
and our food comes often
frozen but in its own shape
(for we hate euphemisms
as you would expect) and our cat's
food comes in tins, other than
scraps of the real thing and she
like a clever cat makes milk
of it for her kittens: we shout
of course but it's electric
like those phantom storms
in the tropics and we think of
the neighbours—I'm not writing
this to say how guilty
we are like some well-paid
theologian at an American
College on a lake
or even to congratulate
the greedy kittens who have
found their mittens and are up
to their eyes in pie—I know
lots of ways of upsetting
God's syllogisms, real
seminar-shakers some of them,
but I'm an historical cat

and I run on rails and so
I don't frame those little poems
which take three lines to
get under your feet—
you know the kind of thing—
The water I boiled the lobster in
is cool enough to top
up the chrysanthemums.
No, I'm acquisitive and have
one hundred and seven Bach
Cantatas at the last count,
but these are things of the spirit
and my wife and our children
and I are animals (biologically
speaking) which is how the world
talks to us, moving on the billiard
table of green London, the sun's
red eye and the cat's green eye
focussing for an end. I know
and you know and we all know
that the certain end of each of us
could be the end of all of us,
but if you asked me what
frightened me most, I wouldn't
say the total bang or even
the circling clot in the red drains
but the picture of a lit room
where two people not disposed
to quarrel have met so
oblique a slant of the dark
they can find no words for
their appalled hurt but only
ride the rearing greyness:
there is convalescence from this,
jokes and love and reassurance,
but never enough and never
convincing and when the cats
come brushing for food their soft

aggression is hateful;
the trees rob the earth and the earth
sucks the rain and the children
burgeon in a time of invalids—
it seems a trio sonata
is playing from a bullock's
skull and the God of Man
is born in a tub of entrails;
all man's regret is no more
than Attila with a cold
and no Saviour here or
in Science Fiction will come
without a Massacre of the Innocents
and a Rape of El Dorado.

KATHLEEN RAINE

The poem to the Daimon I choose because I like it myself,
perhaps for personal reasons. We may use some such
ungainly term as the 'collective unconscious', or the more
ancient 'anima mundi', for what the poem describes, but
the experience is itself as if of a living person with whom
at certain moments we find ourselves in communication.
The visitations of the Daimon are always wonderful. This
is not a literary reason for my liking of the poem, but then
literature is if anything the end, not the origin, of a poem.

'For the Bride' I include for opposite reasons, because
I hope that some readers will like it. It is also of
course about 'anima mundi', though in a rather different
aspect, and one shown more often to the young than to
the old.

∞∞∞∞∞∞

Long ago I thought you young, bright daimon,
Whisperer in my ear
Of springs of water, leaves and song of birds,
By all time younger
Than I, who from the day of my conception
Began to age into experience and pain;
But now life in its cycle swings out of time
    again
I see how old you were,
Older by eternity than I, who, my hair gray,
Eyes dim with reading books,

Can never fathom those grave deep memories
Whose messenger you are,
Day-spring to the young, and to the old,
ancient of days.

For the Bride

I breathed the fragrance of the spray
My mother showed me: 'For the bride.'
'Where does the orange-blossom grow?'
'Not in this country,' she replied,
'But in that other elsewhere land
Some call Spain, some Italy,
Or in marbled orangeries
Where upon branches ever green
Sown thick with buds and opening flowers
Hang golden fruit the leaves below.'

An old lace curtain for a veil,
Crowned with hawthorn, lovely may,
White shells of newly opened flowers,
Heavy anthers ruby-red
Poised on filaments of gold,
A child all day in solemn play
The Bride no bride can ever be,
Yet knew the May Queen was not I,
That none has ever seen Her face
Whom immemorial stories praise,
Bud, and leaf, and blossoming tree.

Modelled in plaster or in wax,
Behind a plate-glass window poised,
Her veil with synthetic garland wreathed,
Aphrodite in her shrine
To whom the passing shop-girls pray

That each some day, one day may be
Beauty upon her bridal-day,
Whose form the image rectifies,
Sweet face and gentle fingers sheathed
Under coarse flesh and common clay.

She is the pang that wounds the heart,
Nuance of consciousness so fine,
Elusive recollection stirred
By scent of syringa in a park,
Or an old Hebridean song,
Lydian or myxolydian mode,
A passing sweetness in the air,
Her still reflection in our dream
With orange or with myrtle crowned,
Whose sacred nuptials are elsewhere.

ANN RIDLER

Because the poem I should choose as my best is too long for this anthology, I single out two which I like for different reasons. In the Villanelle I was for once able to use a highly artificial form to express something which I felt deeply. The two repeated lines in a Villanelle have to be strong enough to bear repetition, and one of them, in this example, has been made to yield slightly different meanings according to its context.

The punning use of the word vessel *was at the source of my second poem—'Choosing a Name'—as well as the more obvious meditation on our strange habit of using, for a new and unknown being, a name that has been owned by others before him. He owns it, or it owns him: 'You and the name exchange a power.' The seam is a rich one, and I think the poem works it thoroughly; moreover, it moves without any waste towards an ending which recalls and completes the thought of the beginning, so that the shape satisfies me.*

‿‿‿‿‿‿

Villanelle for the Middle of the Way

When we first love, his eyes reflect our own;
When mirrors change to windows we can see;
Seeing, we know how much is still unknown.

Was it a trite reflection? What is shown
When we gaze deep begins the mystery:
When we first love, his eyes reflect our own.

Neither of us could cast the first stone,
And to forgive is tender. 'Now,' thought we,
'Seeing, we know.' How much was still unknown

We later learnt. But by forgiveness grown—
As Blake discovered—apt for eternity,
Though in first love his eyes reflect our own.

What was the crime for which you would atone
Or could be crime now between you and me
Seeing we know how much is still unknown?

I know you now by heart not eyes alone,
Dearer the dry than even the green tree.
When we first love, his eyes reflect our own,
Seeing, we know how much is still unknown.

Choosing a Name

My little son, I have cast you out
  To hang heels upward, wailing over a world
  With walls too wide.
My faith till now, and now my love:
  No walls too wide for that to fill, no depth
  Too great for all you hide.

I love, not knowing what I love,
  I give, though ignorant for whom
  The history and power of a name.
I conjure with it, like a novice
  Summoning unknown spirits: answering me
  You take the word, and tame it.

Even as the gift of life
    You take the famous name you did not choose
    And make it new.
You and the name exchange a power:
    Its history is changed, becoming yours,
    And yours by this: who calls this, calls you.

Strong vessel of peace, and plenty promised,
    Into whose unsounded depths I pour
    This alien power;
Frail vessel, launched with a shawl for sail,
    Whose guiding spirit keeps his needle-quivering
    Poise between trust and terror,

And stares amazed to find himself alive;
    This is the means by which you say *I am*,
    Not to be lost till all is lost,
When at the sight of God you say *I am nothing*,
    And find, forgetting name and speech at last,
    A home not mine, dear outcast.

VERNON SCANNELL

'*A Case of Murder*' *is one of those poems that come, alas,
much too infrequently and actually give oneself a surprise.
It comes closest to the kind of poem I most enjoy reading
and trying to write: the one that has an immediately
apprehensible primary meaning or '*plot*' yet offers deeper
and darker levels of significance for the reader who cares
to probe. The poem is about aggression and violence and
the necessity to face the fact that these things exist, yet
there are no abstractions in the poem. It attempts—with
some success I think and hope—to* embody *its theme.*

'*Walking Wounded*' *I like for similar reasons. Also
because it was so damned hard to write. I did—if I remem-
ber rightly—eleven versions of it before I got it to its final
form. The actual visual image of the walking wounded
haunted me for years, long after I had forgotten more
dramatic and spectacular scenes of war. I think I had to
wait so long to write the poem because the merely descrip-
tive poem does not greatly interest me: I had to see what
allegorical or symbolic meaning the image possessed. And
slowly I came to see that the Walking Wounded repre-
sented the common human condition: the dramatically
heroic role is for the few. Most of us have to take the
smaller wounds of living and we have to return again and
again to the battlefield, and perhaps in the long run this
is the more important, even the more heroic role.*

∞∞∞∞

A Case of Murder

They should not have left him there alone,
Alone that is except for the cat.
He was only nine, not old enough
To be left alone in a basement flat,
Alone, that is, except for the cat.
A dog would have been a different thing,
A big gruff dog with slashing jaws,
But a cat with round eyes mad as gold,
Plump as a cushion with tucked-in paws—
Better have left him with a fair-sized rat!
But what they did was leave him with a cat.
He hated that cat; he watched it sit,
A buzzing machine of soft black stuff,
He sat and watched and he hated it,
Snug in its fur, hot blood in a muff,
And its mad gold stare and the way it sat
Crooning dark warmth: he loathed all that.
So he took Daddy's stick and he hit the cat.
Then quick as a sudden crack in glass
It hissed, black flash, to a hiding place
In the dust and dark beneath the couch,
And he followed the grin on his new-made face,
A wide-eyed, frightened snarl of a grin,
And he took the stick and he thrust it in,
Hard and quick in the furry dark,
The black fur squealed and he felt his skin
Prickle with sparks of dry delight.
Then the cat again came into sight,
Shot for the door that wasn't quite shut,
But the boy, quick too, slammed fast the door:
The cat, half-through, was cracked like a nut
And the soft black thud was dumped on the floor.
Then the boy was suddenly terrified
And he bit his knuckles and cried and cried;

But he had to do something with the dead
   thing there.
His eyes squeezed beads of salty prayer
But the wound of fear gaped wide and raw;
He dared not touch the thing with his hands
So he fetched a spade and shovelled it
And dumped the load of heavy fur
In the spidery cupboard under the stair
Where it's been for years, and though it died
It's grown in that cupboard and its hot low purr
Grows slowly louder year by year:
There'll not be a corner for the boy to hide
When the cupboard swells and all sides split
And the huge black cat pads out of it.

Walking Wounded

A mammoth morning moved grey flanks and groaned.
In the rusty hedges pale rags of mist hung;
The gruel of mud and leaves in the mauled lane
Smelled sweet, like blood. Birds had died or flown,
Their green and silent attics sprouting now
With branches of leafed steel, hiding round eyes
And ripe grenades ready to drop and burst.
In the ditch at the cross-roads the fallen rider lay
Hugging his dead machine and did not stir
At crunch of mortar, tantrum of a Bren
Answering a Spandau's manic jabber.
Then into sight the ambulances came,
Stumbling and churning past the broken farm,
The amputated sign-post and smashed trees,
Slow wagonloads of bandaged cries, square trucks
That rolled on ominous wheels, vehicles
Made mythopoeic by their mortal freight
And crimson crosses on the dirty white.

This grave procession passed, though, for a while,
The grinding of their engines could be heard,
A dark noise on the pallor of the morning,
Dark as dried blood; and then it faded, died.
The road was empty, but it seemed to wait—
Like a stage which knows the cast is in the wings—
Wait for a different traffic to appear.
The mist still hung in snags from dripping thorns;
Absent-minded guns still sighed and thumped.
And then they came, the walking wounded,
Straggling the road like convicts loosely chained,
Dragging at ankles exhaustion and despair.
Their heads were weighted down by last night's lead,
And eyes still drank the dark. They trailed the night
Along the morning road. Some limped on sticks;
Others wore rough dressings, splints and slings;
A few had turbanned heads, the dirty cloth
Brown-badged with blood. A humble brotherhood,
Not one was suffering from a lethal hurt,
They were not magnified by noble wounds,
There was no splendour in that company.
And yet, remembering, after eighteen years,
In the heart's throat a sour sadness stirs;
Imagination pauses and returns
To see them walking still, but multiplied
In thousands now. And when heroic corpses
Turn slowly in their decorated sleep
And every ambulance has disappeared
The walking wounded still trudge down that lane,
And when recalled they must bear arms again.

STEVIE SMITH

The metric of 'Angel Boley' interests me very much. The poem needs reading aloud I think to get the swing of the long lines and the sharp break of the shorter ones. It is rather like the tide coming in before an on-shore wind. The story is stern and yet I think merciful, and as what is happening is so terrible, the telling has been keyed down and kept very straightforward. It presents its problems in the words the villagers have chosen—with unerring instinct from Angel's own words—to write on her own tombstone: 'She did evil that good might come.' The better educated vicar, though of excellent heart, is not so 'instinctually' sure as his simpler parishioners. So at first he demurs to the words on the tombstone. But as the story takes its ghostly turn, he sees it is indeed 'the hand of the Lord'. I also like the names very much, though perhaps Boley should be spelt 'Bowley'. But here I was afraid lest some reader, reading it aloud, might hideously say Bowley to rhyme with 'bow-wow'. Perhaps this is being over-anxious. One can so easily be over-anxious and worry poems too much and to no good end.

'The Ass'. I often have the idea in my poems of Death as a friend. Sometimes it is a very buoyant idea of Death. As if he were a god, bringing extreme happiness, opening gates, setting us free. So in this poem, 'The Ass', there is a human being coming at last, through evil, to this extreme happiness. I love this poem for the sense of adventure in it, of a quest and a journey . . . and the girl so protected in her innocence, so 'idle' the world would say, and so happy. I think the line 'Paradise. Paradise' is quite breath-takingly beautiful. I also like the swish and wash of the

sea running in over the saltings and crashing on the sand-
hills of the distant coastline, as it does on the coastline
of North Norfolk by Blakeney Point. How strong this
poem is, how it draws one, how much one wishes to run
with the Ass. And of course again the metric is interest-
ing. The word 'morass' for instance is syncopated where
the stress mark is shown on the first syllable. Only once is
it pronounced in the usual way. I love sometimes to have
the slight use of syncopation.

∞∞∞∞

Angel Boley

There was a wicked woman called Malady Festing
Who lived with her son-in-law, Hark Boley,
And her daughter Angel,
In a house on the high moorlands
Of the West Riding of Yorkshire
In the middle of the last century.

One day Angel
Overheard her mother, Malady, talking to Hark, her
    husband.
Hark, said Malady, it is time
To take another couple of children
Into our kitchen.
Hark laughed, for he too was wicked and he knew
For what purpose the little children
Were required.

But Angel, who was not happy and so
Lived out her life in a dream of absentmindedness,
In order not to be too much aware
Of her horrible relatives, and what it was

That happened every now and then
In the kitchen; and why the children who came
Were never seen again, this time
When she heard what her husband and mother said,
Came out of her absentmindedness and paid attention.
I know now, she said, and all the time I have known
What I did not want to know, that they kill all children
They lure to this house; and that is why, when I pass in
   the village,
The people look askance at me, and they whisper—
But not so that I cannot hear—
There goes the daughter of Mother Lure. And the
   stranger says:
Who is Mother Lure? And they answer: Mrs. Festing
   and they make the sign
That is to protect them from evil. Selfish wretches, said
   Angel,
They do not mind about the children, that evil is not kept
   from *them*.
Angel wandered into the woods, and she said: No more
   children
Are going to be murdered, and before they are murdered,
   tormented
And corrupted; no more children are going to be the
   victims
Of Mother Lure and my husband, Hark. Dark was the
   look then
On Angel's face, and she said: I am the Angel of Death.

Mrs. Festing and Boley
Always left the cooking to Angel, they despised Angel but
   Angel
Could cook, and that they thought was all she was fit for,
To cook and keep house. And they realised
It was far from being to their disadvantage that Angel
   was,
As they thought, half-witted, and never knew
Or wanted to know, what was going on around her.

As soon as Angel
Said to herself: I am the Angel of Death
She became at once very practical and went out into the
woods and fields
And gathered some A. Phalloides, commonly called the
'white' or deadly
Amanita, a mushroom of high toxicity.
These poisonous fungi she put into a soup, and this soup
she gave
To her husband, Hark, and her mother Malady, for
supper, so that they died.
Angel then went to the police and said:
I have done evil, but I have saved many children.

The Judge said: Why did you not tell the police
That children were being destroyed? There was no proof
said Angel,
Because there were no bodies. I never could find out
What they did with the children after they had killed
them.

So then the police searched hard, the wells, the rivers and
the woodlands,
But never could they find out
Where the children lay.

              Nor had the parents of the children
At any time done anything but weep. For they thought
their children
Had been bewitched and done away with, and that
If they told their fears of Mother Lure and her wicked-
ness
To the police, they would not believe them, and more
children than ever
Would disappear.

From then onwards in the trial, Angel spoke
No word more, except to say: I am the Angel of Death.

So they put her in a lunatic asylum, and soon she died
Of an outbreak of typhoid fever. The people of the village
Now loved Angel, because she had delivered them from
    the fear
Of Mother Lure and Hark Boley, and had saved their
Little children from being tormented and slain by these
    wicked people.

So they wrote on her tombstone: 'She did evil that good
Might come.' But the Vicar said it was better not to put
    this
But just her name and age, which was sixteen. So he had
    the words
The villagers had written taken off the tombstone. But
    the next day
The words were again on the tombstone; so again the
    Vicar had them
Removed. And this time a watch was set on the grave,
A police constable and the village sexton watched there
    that night.

And no man came again to write on the tombstone
The forbidden words. Yet when morning came, again
    the words
Were on the tombstone. So the Vicar said: It is the hand
    of the Lord.

And now in that graveyard, at that grave's head beneath
    the yew trees,
Still stands today the tombstone of Angel, with the words
    writ on it:
'She did evil that good might come.' May God be merci-
    ful.

The Ass

In the wood of Wallow
Mash, walked Eugenia, a callow
Girl, they said she was,
An ass.

Beyond the wood there lay a soppy mórass
But the path across was firm, was
Not a-wash.

Three years in the wood Eugenia stayed
By briar and bramble and lost ways
    she was delayed,
And in a witch's house within a thicket
    of yew trees
Was put to work; but seemed so happy
    that the witch
Finding no pleasure in her tyranny
Gave her release
She is an ass, she cried, let her pass
And perish in the soppy mórass.

Eugenia was as happy in the change
To be free to roam and range
As she had been happy and not sad or
    sorry
At her labours in the witch's bothy.

The sun fell hot upon the causeway
That was not very wide
And the mórass sopped and shuffled
Either side.

And the little beetles ran
About, and all the gnats and the mos-
    quitoes sang

And the mórass was as sweet a green
As Eugenia had ever seen.

She sang: Baa-baa-ba-bay
And seven happy years spent on the way.

Once there came a fiend
Who tempted her to go upon the green
Moráss: Come, ass, and go
Upon the green. But she said, No,
She was not such an ass to try the green,
It would deliver her below.

Heigh-ho, heigh-ho,
Never was such a happy idle ass
Since idleness ran glad in Paradise
As Eugenia was.
Paradise. Paradise.

Now the seven years have passed,
The causeway's ended, the soppy mórass
Has sucked its last; the ass
Comes to a sandy pass
Between low sandhills that are tufted
        over with esparto grass,
Beyond, the great seas splash
And roll in pleasure to be so a-wash,
Their white crests coming at a dash
To fetch the ass.

O my poor ass
To run so quickly as if coming home
To where the great waves crash.
Now she is gone. I thought
Into her tomb.

Yet often as I walk that sandy shore
And think the seas

Have long since combed her out that
  lies beneath,
I hear the sweet Ass singing still with
  joy as if
She had won some great prize, as if
All her best wish had come to pass.

STEPHEN SPENDER

'*Nocturne*' *is a reflective poem, a kind of* '*voluntary*' *starting from thoughts about the peace surrounding a child and then travelling out into the world of threats and atomic war. Now I write this note I realize that there must have been at the back of my mind Coleridge's* '*Frost at Midnight*' *which is the classic example of this kind of blank verse slow-paced meditation.*

'*One More New Botched Beginning*' *was written after the death of Louis MacNeice* (*but with the deaths of Merleau-Ponty and Bernard Spencer also in mind*). *The poem is about the way in which poignant memories clutch one by the throat and throw one down into the shrubbery* (*hence the opening lines*).

∞∞∞∞

Nocturne

Their six-weeks-old daughter lies
     in her cot, crying out the night. Their hearts
Are sprung like armies, waiting
To cross the gap to where her loneliness
Lies infinite between them. This child's cry
Sends rays of a star's pain through endless dark;
And the sole purpose of their loving
Is to disprove her demonstration
Of all love's aidlessness. Words unspoken
Out of her mouth unsaying, prove unhappiness

Pure as innocence, virgin of tragedy,
Unknowing reason. Star on star of pain
Surround her cry to make a constellation
Where human tears of victims are the same
As griefs of the unconscious animals.

Listening, the parents know this primal cry
Out of the gates of life, hollows such emptiness,
It proves that all men's aims should be, all times,
To fill the gap of pain with consolation
Poured from the mountain-sided adult lives
Whose minds like peaks attain to heights of snow:
The snow should stoop to wash away such grief.
Unceasing love should lave the feet of victims.

Yet, when they lift their heads out of such truths,
Today mocks at their prayers. To think this even
Suffices to remind them of far worse
Man-made man-destroying ills which threaten
While they try to lull a child. For she
Who cries for milk, for rocking, and a shawl,
Is also subject to the rage of causes
Dividing peoples. Even at this moment
Eyes might fly between them and the moon,
And a hand touch a lever to let fall
That which would make the street of begging roofs
Pulverize and creep skywards in a tower:
Down would fall baby, cradle, and them all.

That which sent out the pilot to destroy them
Was the same will as that with which they send
An enemy to kill their enemy. Even in this love
Running in shoals on each side of her bed,
Is fear, and hate. If they shift their glances
From her who weeps, their eyes meet other eyes
Willed with death, also theirs. All would destroy
New-born, innocent streets. Necessity,
With abstract head and searing feet, men's god

Unseeing the poor amulets of flesh,
Unhearing the minutiae of prayer.

Parents like mountains watching above their
    child,
Envallied here beneath them, also hold
Upon their frozen heights, the will that sends
Destruction into centres of the stones
Which concentrated locked centennial stillness
For human generations to indwell.

Hearing their daughter's cry which is the speech
Of indistinguishable primal life,
They know the dark is filled with means which are
Men's plots to murder children. They know too
No cause is just unless it guards the innocent
As sacred trust: no truth but that
Which reckons this child's tears an argument.

One More New Botched Beginning

Their voices heard, I stumble suddenly,
Choking in undergrowth. I'm torn
Mouth pressed against the thorns,
                                remembering
    Ten years ago here in Geneva,

I walked with Merleau-Ponty by the lake.
Upon his face I saw his intellect.
The energy of the sun-interweaving
Waves, electric, danced on him. His eyes
Smiled with their gay logic through
Black coins thrown down from leaves. He who
Was Merleau-Ponty that day is no more
Irrevocable than the I that day who was
Beside him—I'm still living!

Also that summer
My son stayed up the valley in the mountains.
One day I went to see him, and he stood
Not seeing me, watching some hens.
Doing so, he was absorbed
In their wire-netted world. He danced
On one leg. Leaning forward, he became
A bird-boy. I am there
Still seeing him. To him
That moment—unself knowing even then—
Is drowned in the oblivious earliness. . . .
                              Such pasts
Are not diminished distances, perspective
Vanishing points, but doors
Burst open suddenly by gusts
That seek to blow the heart out. . . .
                              Today, I see
Three undergraduates standing talking in
A college quad. They show each other poems—
Louis MacNeice, Bernard Spencer, and I.
Louis caught cold in the rain, Bernard fell
From a train door.

Their lives are now those poems that were
Pointers to the poems to be their lives.
We read there in the college quad, each poem
Is still a new beginning. If
They had been finished though, they would
        have died
Before they died. Being alive
Is when each moment's a new start, with past
And future shuffled between fingers
For a new game. I'm dealing out
My hand to them, one more new botched
        beginning
There, where we still stand talking in the
        quad.

JON STALLWORTHY

A number of my early poems reflected too faithfully for their own good their maker's lack of involvement in the world around him. They are the poems of an observer rather than a participator, an observer often of other people's lives at moments of crisis. 'The Almond Tree' was one of the first to be written from the inside; it unfolded in my head as the events it described unfolded round me. The early sections were virtually complete before the significance of the tree was made known to me. This fact does not make it a better or a worse poem, but I choose it because it moves with the rhythm of my life and for that reason is important to me.

I choose 'Elm End' as a companion poem to 'The Almond Tree' because it too is concerned with what I have elsewhere described as 'the dynastic theme' and has at its centre the tree image that dominates much of my work. It is, I think, technically the better poem, and since no anthologist has so far chosen it I welcome an opportunity to remedy the oversight.

∽∽∽∽∽

The Almond Tree

I

All the way to the hospital
the lights were green as peppermints.
Trees of black iron broke into leaf
ahead of me, as if

I were the lucky prince
in an enchanted wood
summoning summer with my whistle,
banishing winter with a nod.

Swung by the road from bend to bend,
I was aware that blood was running
down through the delta of my wrist
and under arches
of bright bone. Centuries,
continents it had crossed;
from an undisclosed beginning
spiralling to an unmapped end.

II

Crossing (at sixty) Magdalen Bridge
Let it be a son, a son, said
the man in the driving mirror,
Let it be a son. The tower
held up its hand: the college
bells shook their blessing on his head.

III

I parked in an almond's
shadow blossom, for the tree
was waving, waving me
upstairs with a child's hands.

IV

Up
the spinal stair
and at the top
along
a bone-white corridor
the blood tide swung
me swung me to a room
whose walls shuddered
with the shuddering womb.

Under the sheet
wave after wave, wave
after wave beat
on the bone coast, bringing
ashore—whom?
Just
New-
minted, my bright farthing!
Coined by our love, stamped with
our images, how you
enrich us! Both
you make one. Welcome
to your white sheet,
my best poem!

V

At seven-thirty
the visitors' bell
scissored the calm
of the corridors.
The doctor walked with me
to the slicing doors.
His hand upon my arm,
his voice—*I have to tell
you*—set another bell
beating in my head:
your son is a mongol
the doctor said.

VI

How easily the word went in—
clean as a bullet
leaving no mark on the skin,
stopping the heart within it.

This was my first death.
The 'I' ascending on a slow
last thermal breath
studied the man below

as a pilot treading air might
the buckled shell of his plane—
boot, glove, and helmet
feeling no pain

from the snapped wires' radiant ends.
Looking down from a thousand feet
I held four walls in the lens
of an eye; wall, window, the street

a torrent of windscreens, my own
car under its almond tree,
and the almond waving me down.
I wrestled against gravity,
but light was melting and the gulf
cracked open. Unfamiliar
the body of my late self
I carried to the car.

VII

The hospital—its heavy freight
lashed down ship-shape ward over
    ward—
steamed into night with some on board
soon to be lost if the desperate

charts were known. Others would come
altered to land or find the land
altered. At their voyage's end
some would be added to, some

diminished. In a numbered cot
my son sailed from me; never to come
ashore into my kingdom
speaking my language. Better not

look that way. The almond tree
was beautiful in labour. Blood-

162

dark, quickening, bud after bud
split, flower after flower shook free.

On the darkening wind a pale
face floated. Out of reach. Only when
the buds, all the buds, were broken
would the tree be in full sail.

In labour the tree was becoming
itself. I, too, rooted in earth
and ringed by darkness, from the death
of myself saw myself blossoming,

wrenched from the caul of my thirty
years' growing, fathered by my son,
unkindly in a kind season
by love shattered and set free.

VIII

You turn to the window for the first
    time.
I am called to the cot
to see your focus shift,
take tendril-hold on a shaft
of sun, explore its dusty surface, climb
to an eye you cannot

meet. You have a sickness they cannot
    heal,
the doctors say: locked in
your body you will remain.
Well, I have been locked in mine.
We will tunnel each other out. You
    seal
the covenant with a grin.

In the days we have known one another,
my little mongol love,

I have learnt more from your lips
than you will from mine perhaps:
I have learnt that to live is to suffer,
to suffer is to live.

Elm End

I

Those cherubs on the gate
emasculated by the village boys
are now sole heirs to the estate.

The elms in the avenue,
planted through centuries
one for a daughter, two

for a son, within the year
will carry the timber-
merchant's mark. He walks here

sometimes on Sunday. The rings
on the trunk are numbered:
and a rip-saw sings

in his head seeing columns
of figures march and countermarch.
This Sunday comes

the snow, keeping him indoors:
but it re-vaults the avenue
and for today restores

that manhood the cherubs knew
when a lodge-keeper swung the gate
letting the phaetons through.

II

Don't worry the bell in the porch.
If its tongue is not tied
with rust, it will search

out a ghost from the scullery.
The handle demands both hands:
go in, go up. He will be

pillow-bound in the great bed
under the griffin's eye
that saw his father born, and dead,

and him conceived. His grandmother's
grandmother caged that bird
in its crest, stitching feathers

by candlelight for Charlie
riding to Waterloo.
Under her canopy

the griffin sees not the hollow
trunk, tackled by gravity, but
how far the roots stretch under snow.

III

The fires have fallen. He has drawn
the white acres up to his chin:
fingers grapple the lawn

that once they crawled on. Letting go
can be harder than holding on
or taking hold—as elms ago

the griffin's claw took hold
of these white acres. Letting go
is a language he's too old

to learn. The griffin grips
a scroll inscribed *Hold Fast*
between its talon tips.

Tonight or tomorrow
or tomorrow night
he will cease to echo

the wind in the chimney. Blinds
will be lowered. The snow
will cover his hands.

If then the bulldozer roars
at its kill, he will not hear,
nor see the road-gang's griffin
flex its claws.

R. S. THOMAS

I offer 'Lore' and 'Those Others' both from my third book
Tares. *I would choose these as a reminder of the existence
of* Tares, *which for some reason appears to sell less well
than my other books. Also both these poems are in a regular
stanzaic pattern, which I do not often succeed in writing.
Apart from its concealed pun, 'Lore' sums up fairly well
what I think about the contemporary world, and 'Those
Others' appeals to me as a tribute to a class of people fast
vanishing from Wales, but who have moved me very
strongly.*

∞∞∞∞∞

Lore

Job Davies, eighty-five
Winters old, and still alive
After the slow poison
And treachery of the seasons.

Miserable? Kick my arse!
It needs more than the rain's hearse,
Wind-drawn, to pull me off
The great perch of my laugh.

What's living but courage?
Paunch full of hot porridge,
Nerves strengthened with tea,
Peat-black, dawn found me

Mowing where the grass grew,
Bearded with golden dew.
Rhythm of the long scythe
Kept this tall frame lithe.

What to do? Stay green.
Never mind the machine,
Whose fuel is human souls.
Live large, man, and dream small.

Those Others

A gofid gwerin gyfan
Yn fy nghri fel taerni tân.

Dewi Emrys

I have looked long at this land,
Trying to understand
My place in it—why,
With each fertile country
So free of its room,
This was the cramped womb
At last took me in
From the void of unbeing.

Hate takes a long time
To grow in, and mine
Has increased from birth;
Not for the brute earth
That is strong here and clean
And plain in its meaning
As none of the books are
That tell but of the war

Of heart with head, leaving
The wild birds to sing

The best songs; I find
This hate's for my own kind,
For men of the Welsh race
Who brood with dark face
Over their thin navel
To learn what to sell;

Yet not for them all either,
There are still those other
Castaways on a sea
Of grass, who call to me,
Clinging to their doomed farms;
Their hearts though rough are warm
And firm, and their slow wake
Through time bleeds for our sake.

ANTHONY THWAITE

*Both 'Arabic Script' and 'At Asqefar' were written during
the time I lived in Libya, between 1965 and 1967. 'Arabic
Script' really started, I think, with my hearing an English-
man mockingly describe what Arabic writing looks like—
'as if a spider had been walking through ink'. If you live
in an Arab country such as Libya, naturally you see
Arabic script everywhere—on shop-signs, outside cinemas,
in newspapers. To a westerner, it does seem a very con-
fusing script, full of apparently meaningless squiggles and
dots and dashes: the dots and dashes are known as* dia-
critical *signs, and they indicate accents on vowels. Like
many foreigners, I found them maddeningly difficult to
learn, and though I took Arabic lessons for a while I never
mastered them. To my stupidity, they seemed—and the
whole written language seemed—almost wilfully arbitrary.*

*Yet Arabic—the language of the holy book, the Koran
—was the great force that welded together the Muslim
armies of the seventh century as they poured westward out
of Arabia and all along the North African coast as far as
the Atlantic. The early form of Arabic script is known as
Kufic, and it can still be seen in monumental carvings and
on gravestones: much more firm, angular and strong—
masculine, it seemed to me, as opposed to the feminine
capriciousness of the modern script. I saw such Kufic
carvings at the cemetery of Sidi Kreibish in Benghazi: a
great heap of ancient Muslim graves overtopping the ruins
of the Hellenistic town. They seemed a reflection of the
spirit of the armies of Amr Ibn el-As, which passed this
way with their flags marked with the crescent of Islam:
the 'flaccid colonials' were the feeble Graeco-Roman*

170

settlers who collapsed before them almost without resis-
tance. And the poem grew out of such thoughts. Syntacti-
cally it is a little odd, in that the whole thing consists of
only two sentences.

The place called Asqefar lies about forty miles north-
east of Benghazi; to get there, you have to follow a rough
track across rising country, with juniper and myrtle bushes
all round. When you arrive, there is nothing but a white
zawia *(a small religious centre with a mosque attached)*
and a few Bedouin tents scattered across the hillside.
Here, in what may have been a sanctuary or a tomb or
both, the walls of the cave have been plastered, painted
and glazed; and shining through the glaze are a series of
paintings, some of them concerned with Ulysses and his
return from Troy. The paintings were probably made in
the first or second century A.D.

Very few people ever visit Asqefar or its cave, but there
must have been fighting here, between the Germans and
the British, during the Second World War; and near the
cave I found a bare branch of juniper with a German
soldier's helmet on top of it, and a few scraps of thick grey
material, which may have been part of a German uni-
form. It seemed to mark a grave hurriedly dug for a dead
soldier. When I went there the first time, I asked an Arab
shepherd who was looking after his flocks: 'What hap-
pened here?' All he could say was that there had been
much fighting, much blood. The ancient story of the
Trojan wars and the more recent North African cam-
paigns of the Second World War came oddly and
movingly together in this empty, unvisited landscape. The
remote past, the recent past and the present seemed to flow
together. And the result was this poem, written in 1966,
twenty-five years after the German soldier died and many
centuries after the Trojan wars.

∞∞∞∞∞

Arabic Script

Like a spider through ink, someone says, mocking:
    see it
Blurred on the news-sheets or in neon lights
And it suggests an infinitely plastic, feminine
Syllabary, all the diacritical dots and dashes
Swimming together like a shoal of minnows,
Purposive yet wayward, a wavering measure
Danced over meaning, obscuring vowels and
    breath.
But at Sidi Kreibish, among the tombs,
Where skulls lodge in the cactus roots,
The pink claws breaking headstone, cornerstone,
Each fleshy tip thrusting to reach the light,
Each spine a hispid needle, you see the stern
Edge of the language, Kufic, like a scimitar
Curved in a lash, a flash of consonants
Such as swung out of Medina that day
On the long flog west, across ruins and flaccid
    colonials,
A swirl of black flags, white crescents, a language
    of swords.

At Asqefar

At Asqefar the German helmet
Rests like a scarecrow's bonnet
On a bare branch.
The shreds of coarse grey duffel
Hang round the gap a rifle
Left in a shallow trench.

'Much blood,' said the shepherd,
Gesturing with his head
Towards the bald hillside.

A spent cartridge nestles
Among the dry thistles.
Blood long since dried.

Strange and remote, almost,
As these old figures traced
In Asqefar's cave:
There, pictured in red clay,
Odysseus comes back from Troy
Near the German's grave.

Twenty-five years since the battle
Plucked up the sand and let it settle
On the German soldier.
Far away now the living, the dead,
Disarmed, unhelmeted,
At Troy, at Asqefar.

CHARLES TOMLINSON

For me 'Swimming Chenango Lake' and 'Assassin' form an antithesis, the one an ideal of relationship with the natural world, the other an incident in which all sense of relationship, with man or nature, is betrayed for a political fanaticism.

It is so much a truism one hardly dares repeat it, but since one is misunderstood so often, repetition can perhaps do little harm—by relationship with nature I do not mean 'mere aestheticism', but bringing into play the deepest faculties which, once awakened, are operative and qualitative in all our relationships, human and aesthetic. This is an old truth after all.

'Swimming Chenango Lake' is, by extension, almost an allegory of the way we take purchase on the world of phenomena yet can never 'possess' it, and the way it takes purchase on us, confirming our identity. In 'Assassin' I visualize the denial of relationship, the attempt to go against the grain of humanity and achieve a kind of mystical transcendence by cold will. The incident is the killing of Trotsky. I had in mind also Che Guevara's phrase, 'We must transform ourselves into cold and efficient killing machines.' Since he is so widely and uncritically admired, the moral is self-evident. These two poems, together with another, 'Prometheus', are a trilogy in a sense: they occupy the moral centre of all that I have done. Reviews of The Way of a World *(their context) totally ignored them.*

∽∽∽∽∽∽

Swimming Chenango Lake

Winter will bar the swimmer soon.
    He reads the water's autumnal hesitations
A wealth of ways: it is jarred,
    It is astir already despite its steadiness,
Where the first leaves at the first
    Tremor of the morning air have dropped
Anticipating him, launching their imprints
Outwards in eccentric, overlapping circles.
There is a geometry of water, for this
    Squares off the clouds' redundances
And sets them floating in a nether atmosphere
    All angles and elongations: every tree
Appears a cypress as it stretches there
    And every bush that shows the season,
A shaft of fire. It is a geometry and not
    A fantasia of distorting forms, but each
Liquid variation answerable to the theme
    It makes away from, plays before:
It is a consistency, the grain of the pulsating flow.
    But he has looked long enough, and now
Body must recall the eye to its dependence
    As he scissors the waterscape apart
And sways it to tatters. Its coldness
    Holding him to itself, he grants the grasp,
For to swim is also to take hold
    On water's meaning, to move in its embrace
And to be, between grasp and grasping, free.
    He reaches in-and-through to that space
The body is heir to, making a where
    In water, a possession to be relinquished
Willingly at each stroke. The image he has torn
    Flows-to behind him, healing itself,
Lifting and lengthening, splayed like the feathers
    Down an immense wing whose darkening spread
Shadows his solitariness: alone, he is unnamed

By this baptism, where only Chenango bears a name
In a lost language he begins to construe—
A speech of densities and derisions, of half-
Replies to the questions his body must frame
    Frogwise across the all but penetrable element.
Human, he fronts it and, human, he draws back
    From the interior cold, the mercilessness
That yet shows a kind of mercy sustaining him.
    The last sun of the year is drying his skin
Above a surface a mere mosaic of tiny shatterings,
    Where a wind is unscraping all images in the flowing
        obsidian,
The going-elsewhere of ripples incessantly shaping.

Assassin

The rattle in Trotsky's throat and his wild boar's moans
                                        Piedra de Sol

Blood I foresaw. I had put by
    The distraction of the retina, the eye
That like a child must be fed and comforted
    With patterns, recognitions. The room
Had shrunk to a paperweight of glass and he
    To the centre and prisoner of its transparency.

He rasped pages. I knew too well
    The details of that head. I wiped
Clean the glance and saw
    Only his vulnerableness. Under my quivering
There was an ease, save for that starched insistence
    While paper snapped and crackled as in October air.

Sound drove out sight. We inhabited together
    One placeless cell. I must put down

This rage of the ear for discrimination, its absurd
Dwelling on ripples, liquidities, fact
Fastening on the nerve gigantic paper burrs.
   The gate of history is straiter than eye's or ear's.

In imagination, I had driven the spike
   Down and through. The skull had sagged in its blood.
The grip, the glance—stained but firm—
   Held all at its proper distance and now hold
This autumnal hallucination of white leaves
   From burying purpose in a storm of sibilance.

I strike. I am the future and my blow
   Will have it now. If lightning froze
It would hover as here, the room
   Riding in the crest of the moment's wave,
In the deed's time, the deed's transfiguration
   And as if that wave would never again recede.

The blood wells. Prepared for this
   This I can bear. But papers
Snow to the ground with a whispered roar:
   The voice, cleaving their crescendo, is his
Voice, and his the animal cry
   That has me then by the roots of the hair.

Fleshed in that sound, objects betray me,
   Objects are my judge: the table and its shadow,
Desk and chair, the ground a pressure
   Telling me where it is that I stand
Before wall and window-light:
   Mesh of the curtain, wood, metal, flesh:

A dying body that refuses death,
   He lurches against me in his warmth and weight,
As if my arm's length blow
   Had transmitted and spent its strength
Through blood and bone; and I, spectred,
   The body that rose against me were my own.

177

Woven from the hair of that bent head,
   The thread that I had grasped unlabyrinthed all—
Tightrope of history and necessity—
   But the weight of a world unsteadies my feet
And I fall into the lime and contaminations
   Of contingency; into hands, looks, time.

TED WALKER

It's hard to choose, but I suppose I have a special affection for 'Easter Poem' in Fox on a Barn Door *and 'Swallows' in my new book* The Night Bathers.

First, 'Easter Poem'. For as long as I remember I have written poetry, but it wasn't until I was about 28 years old that I did so professionally; *as the central activity in my life, I mean, not for money! This was among the first poems I wrote, then, to be seen in public. While it was being made I discovered how immensely difficult the craft of poetry is, and to what extent an artist depends on some measure of good luck—recognizing the happy accident, that is, and turning it to his advantage. In this poem, which began as a simple descriptive piece about the stretched fox, the accident took the form of those bits of burdock snagged in the animal's fur; I recognized the Crown of Thorns in them and at once realized that the image of the fox had troubled me, not because of its horror, but because it had reminded me of the crucifixion and my dying faith in Christianity. I discovered that, for me, a poem is not so much a means of saying what I think as finding out what I knew only dimly to be on my mind. If I already know what I want to say, I don't bother trying to make a poem of it; there's no mystery left, and therefore no interest to me. I found all this out in 'Easter Poem' and, vitally important, I discovered the sound of my true voice. When it was finished, I knew at once that it was the real thing, that this was what I'd always do, and that if I ever published a book it would be called* Fox on a Barn Door. *That title always serves to*

179

remind me that it is the image that I must be concerned with, not the idea.

'Swallows' I like because it celebrates a brief period of total happiness in my life. It speaks of inner prosperity, of material sufficiency, and was written when I was able to give up teaching and spend my time waiting for poems to turn up. I was able to buy a house where there were swallows building; they were there, symbols of my contentment, and I could neither ensure their staying nor prevent them coming again. And I like the texture of the poem, the richness of its images, its accuracy.

In both poems there are terrible weaknesses which I don't think I can do anything about. They were damned hard work and left me spent. I have the feeling that, in years to come, I'll be able to read them and say, 'Yes, that's just how it was.'

One last thing. It has been suggested that the poems I choose 'may say something which particularly needs saying today'. That is the very last consideration as far as I'm concerned. 'Today' is not a word for a poet.

∽∽∽∽∽

Easter Poem

I had gone on Easter Day
early and alone to be
beyond insidious bells
(that any other Sunday
I'd not hear) up to the hills
where are winds to blow away

commination. In the frail
first light I saw him, unreal
and sudden through lifting mist,
a fox on a barn door, nailed

like a coloured plaster Christ
in a Spanish shrine, his tail

coiled around his loins. Sideways
his head hung limply, his ears
snagged with burdock, his dry nose
plugged with black blood. For two days
he'd held the orthodox pose.
The endemic English noise

of Easter Sunday morning
was mixed in the mist swirling
and might have moved his stiff head.
Under the hill the ringing
had begun: and the sun rose red
on the stains of his bleeding.

I walked the length of the day's
obsession. At dusk I was
swallowed by the misted barn,
sucked by the peristalsis
of my fear that he had gone,
leaving nails for souvenirs.

But he was there still. I saw
no sign. He hung as before.
Only the wind had risen
to comb the thorns from his fur.
I left my superstition
stretched on the banging barn door.

Swallows

A day of winter-slaked April.
Bobbers on a wire at a wall—
trindles of fire-blued iron
that any wind twitches—twirl
and are lifted into swallows.

Little particles of thirst,
the red of summer brickdust
are those throats among a month
avaricious of its damp; fust
of the whitening lichen,

buffed by delicate bellies,
comes live out of its ice.
Blue is warm of swallows' wings:
rich spillings of their sapphires
glint along the dark, nettled end

of garden. They are my claim—
over half a world they come,
crop-full of Africa, to lodge
in crevices of my home.
In honorance of such plenty,

I make them a plot of hotness
to skim upon: hibiscus,
hyssop, pools of buddleia,
a humming of mulberries.
I fork the brown mulch of one

summer less into my earth
as warm weather falls. Noth-
ing can encourage their coming
again. I leave them be, with
an untouched, vulnerable clutch

of another year's small flesh.
Soon my eyes must relinquish
them. When the hips are redder
than the roses were, they'll brush
my willow a final time,

flying out of the house.
And, a continent deep, I sense
some other self—between us,
paltry, diminishing oceans
and arid, vanishing land.

Kraaled in a vast and untreed
veld, his sleep is troubled.
My wall of lichen relapses white.
In the night he lifts his head,
listening for ultimate swallows.

BIOGRAPHICAL NOTES

Dannie ABSE was born in 1923 in Cardiff where he went to school and began his medical studies at the Welsh National School of Medicine. Later, he completed his medical studies at Westminster Hospital, London. He now lives in that city where he thinks of himself as a part-time doctor and a professional poet. He has published five books of poems, one of the most recent being *Selected Poems*.

Kingsley AMIS was born in 1922 and educated at the City of London School and St John's College, Oxford. After serving in the Army he lectured at the University College of Swansea until with growing success as a novelist he was able to devote his time to writing. His books of verse include *A Case of Samples* and *A Look Round the Estate*.

W. H. AUDEN was born in York in 1907 and educated at Gresham's School, Holt, and Christ Church, Oxford. He was awarded the King's Medal for Poetry in 1937 and has published many books of verse, plays and criticism. His latest book of verse is *City Without Walls*.

Sir John BETJEMAN was born in 1906 and educated at Marlborough and Oxford. He is an authority on church architecture, Victorian architects and on topographical subjects. His *Collected Poems*, published in 1958, sold more than 100,000 copies in six months. Among his other books of verse are *High and Low* and a verse autobiography, *Summoned by Bells*. He is the present Poet Laureate, appointed in 1972.

Thomas BLACKBURN was born in Cumberland in 1916. He is at present lecturing at the College of St Mark and St

John in London. Before that he taught in various schools and for two years was Gregory Fellow of Poetry at Leeds University. He has published six books of verse, including *A Smell of Burning* and *The Fourth Man*, an autobiographical study, two volumes of criticism, and a novel.

Edmund BLUNDEN was born in 1896 and educated at Christ's Hospital and the Queen's College, Oxford. He published *Undertones of War*, based upon his experiences in the 1914–18 war, in 1928. His life has been spent in writing and teaching and he was awarded the Hawthornden Prize in 1922. His books of verse include *After the Bombing*, *The Midnight Skaters* and *Poems of Many Years*.

Alan BROWNJOHN was born in 1931 and educated at London primary and grammar schools and at Merton College, Oxford. He was a teacher for twelve years and now lectures at Battersea College of Education. His books include *Sandgrains on a Tray*, *Warrior's Career*, *Brownjohn's Beasts* and *To Clear the River*.

Charles CAUSLEY was born in 1917 at Launceston in Cornwall where he still writes and teaches and has lived all his life apart from six years in the wartime Royal Navy. He has published seven books of verse and was awarded the Queen's Medal for Poetry in 1967 and a Cholmondeley Award for Poetry in 1971. Recent collections of his verse are *Underneath the Water*, *Figure of 8* and *Figgie Hobbin*.

Richard CHURCH was born in London in 1893 and educated at Dulwich Hamlet School. He worked in the Civil Service until 1933 when he took up full-time writing. His books of verse include *The Inheritors* and *The Burning Bush*. He died in 1971.

Patric DICKINSON was born in 1914 and educated at St Catharine's College, Cambridge, where he took a degree in Classics and English. After teaching for three years he was severely injured in training for the Army in 1940. Later he worked for the B.B.C. as writer and producer, and he won the Atlantic Award in Literature in 1948. Latterly he has free-lanced. His books of verse include *This Cold Universe* and *Selected Poems.*

Lawrence DURRELL was born in India in 1912 and educated at St Edmund's School, Canterbury. He describes himself as belonging to India by birth, Ireland by parentage, Great Britain by citizenship, and the Mediterranean by preference. After having failed to enter Cambridge he took on many odd jobs including that of jazz pianist in a night-club. He has written novels, among them *The Alexandria Quartet*, and his books of verse include *Selected Poems* (1957) and *Collected Poems* (1960). He now lives in Provence.

Clifford DYMENT was born in 1914 in Derbyshire and educated at Loughborough Grammar School. His books of verse include *The Axe in the Wood, Poems 1935–1948* and *Experiences and Places.* He died in 1971.

Roy FULLER was born in 1912, worked for many years as a solicitor and is now Professor of Poetry at Oxford. Since his *Collected Poems 1936–61* he has published three collections of poems, *Buff, New Poems,* and *Seen Grandpa Lately?*

Robert GITTINGS was born in 1911 and educated at Cambridge University, where he studied History. He is a poet, biographer and playwright, and his books of verse include *Matters of Love and Death* and *American Journey.*

Robert GRAVES was born in 1895 in London and educated at Charterhouse and St John's College, Oxford. He served in the 1914–18 war and he has lived by writing since publishing his autobiographical *Goodbye to All That* in 1929. His most recent books of verse are *Poems 1965–1968,* and *Poems 1968–1970.*

Thom GUNN was born in 1929 in Gravesend and educated at Cambridge. He has lived in San Francisco for most of the last 17 years and teaches at the University of California. His most recent book of verse is *Moly.*

Seamus HEANEY was born in 1939 and educated at St Columb's College, Derry, and Queen's University, Belfast, where, after a period of teaching in schools, he now lectures. His books of verse include *Death of a Naturalist*, *Door into the Dark* and *Wintering Out*.

John HEATH-STUBBS was born in 1918 in London and read English at the Queen's College, Oxford. He worked in London for a short time as a schoolmaster and publishers' hack. He was Gregory Fellow of Poetry at Leeds University 1952–55 and subsequently held Visiting Professorships in Egypt and America. At present he lectures at the College of St Mark and St John in London. His books of verse include *Selected Poems* and *Artorius*.

Philip HOBSBAUM is of Russian-Jewish ancestry and was born in London in 1932. He was educated in Yorkshire and at Cambridge, and after acquiring a doctorate at the University of Sheffield taught for some years at Queen's University, Belfast. He now lectures at the University of Glasgow. His books of verse include *Coming Out Fighting* and *Women and Animals*.

David HOLBROOK was born in Norwich in 1923 and read English at Cambridge. He has worked in adult education and taught in school and university. His published work includes a novel, several books on education and criticism, numerous school books, a libretto and five books of verse, the most recent being *Object Relations* and *Old World, New World*.

Ted HUGHES was born in 1930 in Yorkshire where he attended Mexborough Grammar School. He took his degree at Pembroke College, Cambridge, and after that has lived mainly from his writing, with spells of teaching in the United States. He now lives in Devon. His recent books of verse include *Wodwo* and *Crow*.

Elizabeth JENNINGS was born in 1926 and educated at Oxford High School and St Anne's College, Oxford. Her books of verse include *The Mind Has Mountains* and *Collected Poems* (1967).

187

James KIRKUP was born in 1923 in Co. Durham. He was educated at local schools and at King's College, Newcastle upon Tyne. He describes himself as 'a poet of many styles and subjects, from formal odes to Japanese and Korean forms'. He has taught in many countries and has recently spent several years lecturing in Japan. His publications include travel books, novels, translations, plays and books of poetry. His most recent books of verse are *White Shadows, Black Shadows* and *The Body Servant*.

Philip LARKIN was born in 1922 in Coventry and went to St John's College, Oxford. He is now Librarian of the University of Hull. His publications include *The Less Deceived* and *The Whitsun Weddings*. In 1965 he was awarded the Queen's Medal for Poetry

Laurie LEE was born in 1914 in the Cotswolds and began writing poetry at the local village school. On leaving school at fifteen he had a number of jobs and spent a year travelling in Spain and earning his keep by playing a violin in the streets. In addition to his highly successful autobiographical *Cider with Rosie* he has published several books of verse including *The Sun My Monument* and *My Many-Coated Man*.

C. Day LEWIS was born in Ballintubber in Eire in 1904 and educated at Sherborne School and Wadham College, Oxford. After several years of teaching he took up full-time writing, lecturing and broadcasting. He published novels, translations, critical works and poetry. His *Collected Poems* were published in 1954 and he was appointed Poet Laureate in 1968. He died in 1972.

Edmund LUCIE-SMITH was born in Jamaica in 1933 and educated at King's School, Canterbury, and Merton College, Oxford. He has worked in advertising and as a free-lance journalist and broadcaster. His books of verse include *A Tropical Childhood*.

George MacBETH was born at Shotts in Scotland in 1932. He was educated at King Edward VII School, Sheffield, and New College, Oxford. He has worked as an editor and producer with the BBC and is the author of several books. His most recent books of verse are *The Night of Stones* and *A War Quartet*.

Roger McGOUGH was born in Liverpool in 1937 and educated at St Mary's College, Crosby, and Hull University. He has been a teacher and lecturer and now earns his living by writing and working with 'The Scaffold'. His books of verse include *Watchwords* and *After the Merrymaking*.

Norman NICHOLSON was born in 1914 at Millom, Cumberland, in the house where he still lives. His native region was the main source of the imagery for his first three books of verse, the best of which can be read in *Selected Poems*. His most recent book of verse is *A Local Habitation*.

Brian PATTEN was born in Liverpool in 1946. He left school at fourteen and worked for a local newspaper. He now lives largely on money from poetry readings and from his writing. His books of verse include *Little Johnny's Confession*, *Notes to the Hurrying Man* and *The Irrelevant Song*.

Ruth PITTER was born at Ilford in 1897 and educated at the Coborn School, Bow. Her books of verse include *Still by Choice* and *Poems 1922–66*.

William PLOMER was born in South Africa in 1903 and educated at Rugby School. He has written a great many books, including novels, short stories, biography and poetry, and has recently acted as a librettist to Benjamin Britten. His *Collected Poems* were published in 1960.

Peter PORTER was born in Australia in 1929. He was educated locally and worked in Brisbane as a journalist until coming to England in 1951. His life since then has been devoted to writing poetry and supporting himself by such jobs as clerking, book selling and advertising writing. He is now a free-lance writer in journals and on the BBC. His recent books of verse include *A Porter Folio*, *The Last of England* and *Preaching to the Converted*.

Kathleen RAINE was born in 1908 and educated at Girton College, Cambridge, where she took her degree in Natural Science. Her most recent volumes of verse are *The Hollow Hill* and *The Lost Country*.

Anne RIDLER was born in 1912 at Rugby and educated at Downe House School and King's College, London. She has published plays, biography and poems. Her books of verse include *A Matter of Life and Death* and *Selected Poems* (1961).

Vernon SCANNELL was born in 1922 and educated at elementary schools and for one year at Leeds University. He was wounded in the 1939–45 war and for a while boxed as a professional and travelled with a fairground booth. He has published novels as well as six books of verse. His *The Masks of Love* won the Heinemann Award for Literature in 1960. His most recent publications are *Selected Poems* and an autobiography, *The Tiger and the Rose*.

Stevie SMITH was born in 1902 in Hull and was educated at Palmer's Green High School and the North London Collegiate School. She was awarded the Queen's Medal for Poetry in 1969 and died in 1971. Her books of verse include *Not Waving but Drowning* and *Selected Poems* (1962).

Stephen SPENDER was born in 1909 and educated at University College School and University College, Oxford. He has travelled widely and lectured in many parts of the world. In addition to his poetry he has written a play, a novel, short stories and much criticism. His books of verse include *Collected Poems* (1954) and *Selected Poems* (1965).

Jon STALLWORTHY was born in 1935 of New Zealander parents. He was educated at Rugby, in the Royal West

African Frontier Force, and at Magdalen College, Oxford, where he won the Newdigate Prize for poetry in 1958. He has published books of criticism and four books of verse, the most recent being *Root and Branch* and *Positives*.

R. S. THOMAS was born in 1913 at Cardiff and was educated at the University of Wales. He was subsequently ordained and is now Vicar of Aberdaron in Caernarvonshire. Among his most recent books of verse are *Pietà* and *Not That He Brought Flowers*.

Anthony THWAITE was born in 1930 at Chester and was educated at Kingswood School, Bath, and Christ Church, Oxford. He has taught in universities in Japan and Libya, and has worked in the BBC and as a literary editor. His books of poems include *The Owl in the Tree*, *The Stones of Emptiness* and *Inscriptions*.

Charles TOMLINSON was born in 1927 at Stoke-on-Trent and was educated at Queens' College, Cambridge. He is now Reader in English Poetry at the University of Bristol. His books include *A Peopled Landscape*, *The Way of a World* and *Written on Water*.

Ted WALKER was born at Lancing in 1934. He was educated at Steyning Grammar School and St John's College, Cambridge, where he took a degree in Modern Languages. His books of verse include *Fox on a Barn Door*, which won the Eric Gregory Award for 1964, and *The Night Bathers*.